THE PROBLEM WITH IMMIGRANTS

THE PROBLEM WITH IMMIGRANTS

Derek Laud

Biteback Publishing

First published in Great Britain in 2015 by
Biteback Publishing Ltd
Westminster Tower
3 Albert Embankment
London SE1 7SP
Copyright © Derek Laud 2015

ISBN 978-1-84954-721-5

10 9 8 7 6 5 4 3 2 1

A CIP catalogue record for this book is available from the British Library.

Set in Adobe Garamond Pro

Printed and bound in Great Britain by
CPI Group (UK) Ltd, Croydon CR0 4YY

To Anne, Pat, Cicely and Charles. Thank you all for your love and support.

Then there is Ceeker too. She is the leading lady in my life and the most beautiful Jack Russell I have ever owned.

With love,

Derek

January 2015

Contents

Preface: Enoch Powell

HIS VERY NAME HAS SOMETHING of a menacing ring about it. Enoch Powell – or, to be more precise, John Enoch Powell – was a menace. He spent thirty-seven years as a Member of Parliament and three years as Minister of Health – and he was a menace to many of his colleagues. This classical scholar, author, poet, politician and, in his time, the youngest brigadier in the British Army died in 1998. It is doubtful that he will be remembered for any of those exceptional things … bar one, perhaps. It was as a politician – a Tory politician – that he made his indelible mark. Speaking in 1990 in Cambridge, he said: 'I was born a Tory, I am a Tory … it is part of me, it's something I cannot change' – but he died without a Tory membership card in his wallet. Oddly enough, though, it was not the issue of race and immigration – for which he became best known – that caused the parting of the waves.

When I first heard the word 'racist', it was in connection with Enoch Powell. I was about eight years old at the time and, long before I knew much about anything else, I knew about Enoch Powell. I remember seeing a photograph of him. He looked intense. There was no smile. I was curious.

Politics was everything to Powell. Many think that, had it not been for the 1968 'Rivers of Blood' speech, he would have been Prime Minister. I do not subscribe to that view myself. Powell was not temperamentally suited to office: he was a loner and could not live side by side with collective responsibility. He always needed to be right. He was also in a party, as Lord Hailsham once put it, 'that thinks it is wicked to have brains'. For that reason too, he was always going to be the odd man out.

This isn't a book about Powell, and I cannot give any authoritative judgement of him (I did not know him well enough). My contribution is as a bystander – who witnessed, for over a decade, many of his orations from the gallery of the House of Commons – and as an earnest young researcher – who pored over many of his past speeches and articles. There was no doubting that the man was a Tory to his fingertips.

However, the very thing Powell said – he was born a Tory – was in fact something he spent most of his lifetime opposing. He started early, resigning from Macmillan's government over public expenditure in 1958. Then, and most infamously, came his views on immigration and 'Rivers of Blood'. And subsequently, almost as if he were working to a deliberate ten-year cycle, the Common Market reared its head and he voted Labour in the 1974 general election as a result. He was always drifting against the prevailing tide, and there were other policy differences too.

Many thought of Powell as a dangerous figure. To them, he had too many principles (the Conservatives had always been largely pragmatic until Mrs Thatcher came along) and he seemed hell-bent on destroying his party if he could not make it in his own image. When he famously urged the voter to turn on the Tory Party and vote Labour in 1974, he created a rift he could not have known would be permanent. Powell had in fact previously voted Labour in the 1945 general election, because he had wanted to punish the Conservative Party for the Munich Agreement.

Indeed, in my view, he was not – by any means – always wrong in his endeavours to reprimand his party. I personally hate the chant 'my party, right or wrong, my party'.

All political parties need fearless figures like Powell. I was so admiring of him – and Tony Benn – for that same reason: the political stage is dull without them, and there are no comparable figures today. All good revolutions are intellectual and Powell provided his fair share of revolutions. We all remember Winston Churchill for his leadership during the Second World War, but, like Powell, he was independent-minded and he even changed party too. In fact, in a quote never published before – but kindly made available to me by the Trustees of the Gilmour family – Churchill had similar concerns about immigration. This is taken from Lord Gilmour's unpublished diaries:

> The next week we had a rather different social occasion, this time, no doubt, at the instance of Caroline's mother. She and we were invited to lunch at 10 Downing Street with only the Prime Minister, his wife Lady Churchill, his daughter Mary Soames, and his private secretary Jock Colville. Although very deaf to begin with, Sir Winston became much less so after he had summoned his hearing aid, and he was as far from being gaga as anybody else present. He was given frequent messages as to how questions were proceeding in the Commons. In those days, Prime Minister's questions did not begin at a set time, but only if, and when, ordinary questions reached no. 45. On our day, they didn't. After a while Churchill raised the question of *The Spectator*'s attitude to the arrival of immigrants from the West Indies. I explained our fears that if immigration continued at its current rate there would be an explosion in Brixton or elsewhere; we therefore favoured measures to restrict it. After expressing some measure of approval, the Prime Minister said: 'I think it is the most important subject facing this country, but I cannot get any of my ministers to take any notice.'

It was a spring day on 20 April 1968 when Enoch Powell rose to his feet to deliver what might very well be the most famous and controversial speech ever made on race relations and immigration in Britain. Ever since that time, Powell's name has been synonymous with immigration and, in particular, with racism. It is not hard to see how this impression came about. To re-read his speech is a chilling experience. To watch the video footage is distressing. The language, the intonations and the intensity are nothing short of deliberate histrionics. His small frame, pearl-like blue eyes and nasal tones make this man intriguing from the off.

An examination of the original typed text of his speech – with additions and corrections in his own hand (complete with underlining of points to emphasise) – implies, as one would expect from him, preparedness for the storm he was about to create. He must have known that he was gambling his entire career and reputation on this one speech. Powell knew what he was about – I can't imagine he ever had much self-doubt – and he intended his contribution to be disruptive and offensive. But to whom? Was he really targeting the Afro-Caribbean community (as Churchill clearly was), or the leader of his own party (whom he desperately wanted to destabilise, if not replace)? Could Heath really have been the intended victim? I have no doubt that, among many things, Powell knew how to be Machiavellian.

Churchill died three years before Powell's speech, but they would have sat in the Commons together. Powell would seemingly have enjoyed support from Churchill for his concern about immigration, but I doubt for his use of emotive and vulgar language. The ghost of Enoch Powell looms large whenever I think of immigration, and surely it is the same for others of my generation? The unsettled question (for me, certainly) wasn't whether Powell was wrong or right – broadly speaking, he was wrong (of that, I am sure) – but rather whether his motives were racialist or not. On that, I just cannot be forthcoming. There are others who are more certain: I argued with the late James Baldwin about it into the early hours while staying with him in France. If he could not persuade me, then I doubt anyone else can.

Powell's influence rapidly waned after 1968 and it was in 1974 that he made his next major move: he resigned from the Tory Party and stood for the Ulster Unionists in an election in the Northern Ireland seat of South Down.

The menace in Powell surfaced on the political landscape in a major way – across the board and always unpredictably. We shared John Biffen in common as friends. I adored John and miss him very much – this urbane, intellectual and witty man had a considerable influence on my outlook. He once described Enoch as being 'a fully paid-up member of the awkward squad'. I think he was being characteristically kind to his friend.

Jim Prior amusingly dubbed Powell the 'Wolverhampton Wanderer'. Prior didn't trust Powell and hostilities intensified during the former's period as Northern Ireland Secretary. To be frank, Powell was downright stubborn. He was egotistical and, yes, fearless to the point of wilful destruction. He was also clearly riddled with integrity and was a passionate parliamentarian. Britain is a much safer place when our elected politicians have a disposition towards a parliamentary conscious, and Powell did – I will always salute that.

Powell raises more questions to which I *can* provide answers. I was once, like Powell, a man for whom politics was everything. I admired him from afar. I have always been economically Powellite, but departed from the manner in which he expressed his views: I don't believe in using fear as a justification for policy-making, which is what he was doing in his 1968 speech. That is also what our current second-tier politicians do while snatching our liberties from under our noses as if it were a plaything. The dangerously ambitious and suspect Home Secretary Theresa May is one to be watched.

What would Powell make of today's London, a financial capital of the world economically fuelled by a significantly foreign workforce? The company where I am a partner employs people from at least twelve different nationalities; between us, we speak eighteen different languages. Our capital city is diverse and we are benefitting from such diversity in many ways, not just economically.

I wish I had made more effort to get to know him, but I suspect that would have been in vain. Powell and I first eyed each other in the 'corridors of power'. We were on nodding terms long before we actually spoke. We tipped hats towards each other outside the Houses of Parliament on early winter mornings, and, although I had heard stories about how notoriously difficult Powell was with small talk, that didn't deter me – I wanted to meet him. Something told me the moment would come. I brushed up on my Latin and Ancient Greek (with Cicely's invaluable help and patience) in readiness for the occasion. When the moment arrived, I was seated on the right of Powell and we were breaking bread on a long table. Enoch Powell was in talkative mood. He asked about my ancestry and my route into politics. We spoke about horse riding and our shared passion for hunting. I felt no nervousness – in stark contrast to expectation. I made no slip of the tongue and felt I came through the experience unscathed. I will never know what he made of me, but I long ago gave up caring what others think.

Trying to fathom what was in Powell's highly intellectual mind when he combined crude language – 'grinning picaninnies' – with the majesty of classical citations – 'like the Roman, I seem to see the river Tiber foaming with much blood' – remains an unresolved question, even more than forty-six years later. The explicit target and excuse he gave for his speech was the impending Race Relations Bill. The clause that related to the racial discrimination provision was in his sights, and he didn't like it. He implied there was no need for anti-discriminatory laws. It's important to remember the time and context in which he was making this speech: Britain was, and still is now, an overwhelmingly white Anglo-Saxon nation. He was speaking for the majority, as he saw it. However, to my mind, this did not justify the use of exaggerated

metaphors. It is astonishing that he seemed not to attach suffi-
cient importance to the sensitivity his subject matter required.
I see a reoccurrence of this today. Michael Fallon, the usually
sure-footed Cameron foot-soldier, reignited the 'swamping'
metaphor in the same terms as Margaret Thatcher did in the
1987 general election. It seems all Tory leaders feel the same
about immigration. John Major, the man from south London
(for whom I worked), couldn't resist making immigration an
issue in his 1992 general election campaign. I had expected
better from John.

Powell's speech was excessively gloomy on immigration.
Broadly speaking, he might have been right about the numbers here in today's terms, but he was wrong to forecast the
'foaming of much blood'. His predictions of racial riots simply have not materialised. He failed to completely understand
that integration could work (although, in fairness, he did say
it was not impossible), or that tolerance was much more in
the human grain than racial hatred or community conflict.
I personally have found this to be true. I have enjoyed both
a rural and urban upbringing. I felt at home in both places,
although the differences between rural and urban communities
are vast. In Suffolk, Norfolk, Hampshire, Leicestershire – to
name some of the rural parts of England I have lived in or
visited regularly – I was always made to feel welcome. Indeed,
the Italian who was a finalist in last year's *X Factor* reminded
us every week that we have made him feel just the same.

In 1988, I was asked to judge the bonny pony competition

while staying with friends in Lincolnshire. There were at least thirty entries coming from places far and wide. I gave first prize – and the obligatory rosette – to a boy who must have been all of five years old. I suspect it was the first time he had ever seen a black man, some twenty years after Enoch's speech. I doubt much has changed in Lincolnshire since that visit and I doubt the existence of a black person in that village today. I trust that boy is now a successful young man in gainful employment. I hope he will remember me for awarding him his first ever rosette. I forget his name now, but I think he might have been a John. Entirely unbeknown to me, I had just given the Rt Hon. John Enoch Powell's grandson first prize. The irony has kept me giggling to this day, even if my parents can't quite share in the laugh.

Powell colours the race debate, even now. Many today are striking Powellesque poses, even if they may baulk at being called Powellite. But he is not the reason I have written this book – that is better explained in the first chapter – rather it is the writing of this book that puts me in mind of him again. It would have been marvellous to have asked him to write this preface for himself, so writing about him is the next best thing.

But now that I *am* thinking about him, what interests me today is the fact he changed his party. I take a little satisfaction from the thought that Enoch Powell and I – for very different reasons – both spoke out when we needed to, and were not afraid to move on. If only I could speak to him again…

Chapter 1

Surfing the wave

EVER SINCE I WAS YOUNG, certain phrases have been ringing in my ears, ringing like ritual incantations: 'bloody foreigners'; 'send them back'; and, most common of all, 'the problem with immigration'. It is the nature of these incantations – in fact the very point of them – that they trip off the tongue almost without consciousness; sacred, reassuring truisms rubbed through repetition into the way of the world, day after delusional day.

The perception that I had – that any young black person could have – was that 'we' were a problem. Maybe even *the* problem. It's no wonder that integration came so hard, especially for those arrivals from the New Commonwealth. Britons talk as if this ancient island has had little or no immigration until relatively recently. This is, of course, untrue.

In this book I will retell the story ... many stories, in fact – some anecdotal and many more factual – as a personal survey of Britain's long and almost ancient history of introducing foreigners to our shores.

This is not an autobiography, but a few words of personal introduction are probably in order. I was born of Jamaican and Indian heritage. My father is half-Indian. My parents came to England from Jamaica in 1960 when they were in their early thirties.

In the idyllic rural Jamaican parish of St Catherine's, they had a substantial house in the mountains and were the owners of a thriving family farming business. My father's family were living a comfortable existence. One day, believing what they had heard, they embarked on a world-shattering journey. They precariously boarded a plane for the first time in their lives. What my parents left behind was considerable, but the sense of future 'gains' persuaded them to make the journey. They both came with much trepidation in their hearts and it was said you could hear it in their voices too.

Immaculately dressed and handsome in looks, the newlyweds were horrified by, as well as out of place in, the 'ugly', styleless urban jungle of post-war London. The rural life they had loved – in a village mainly comprising small cottages painted in clashing colours of bright red, yellow and green – was nowhere to be seen on London's Clapham Common. They knew few people here and only one of their relatives followed them.

My uncle was a teacher in Jamaica (his son is now a professor in the United States) and there he stayed, despite temptations from the British government to lure him to their own island life. He held the view then that the education system in the UK would not be as good as the schools in his own country or as beneficial to the immigrant communities. He was a man of extraordinary foresight. Today, more and more Afro-Caribbean children are being sent to Caribbean islands for their education because their parents have completely lost faith in British education – here, they might easily leave school unable to speak English properly, read, write or do simple arithmetic. Many immigrants who came from the New Commonwealth were university-educated and qualified professional people, especially in the field of medicine, although this made no difference to their job prospects in post-war Britain. They found obstacles put in their way when applying for professional posts. They were employed for manual work and mainly in the lower echelons of the health service or nationalised industries. So many more stayed in the Caribbean than left for Britain.

For those who did come, it took them a long while to settle. Life was hard, cold and grey – like someone had switched off all the lights – even at midday. All they ever longed for was to return home to their missing loved ones. As this book will explain, the vast majority of post-war immigrants from the West Indian sub-continent had never intended to stay, but Harold Macmillan, unintentionally, made it difficult for them to return.

My own grandparents I did not know – they never came to

England. I only know them through stories and photographs as I never went to Jamaica in their lifetime. But it was not long before I was to find a new family and one that included a 'Granny'. The greatest influences on my early life came from Anne and Cicely Meehan. I have known them since the age of three years old. They taught me the values of hard work and compassion. Anne is a lifelong socialist and Cicely a liberal intellectual. They boxed my ears when I placed a Conservative poster in the front room window with Margaret Thatcher's face on it. We had achieved a 'balanced' ticket in our house, and one of my childhood memories is learning the fine art of how to disagree without falling out.

These two white sisters never married, and they were pillars of the local community. Church, work and 'Love thy neighbour' is how they led their lives – and still do today. Cicely read Classics at university and Anne was a music scholar, as well as my first teacher. I spent much of my time with them and became an 'adopted' member of the family. I cannot forget Patricia (Pat) – she was the youngest of the three sisters but got married in the 1970s to a leading surgeon, who later became a Professor of Medicine at Cairo University. I loved her letters from Egypt; she had a grand life, moving among the intellectual elite and a house staffed by 'servants'. The sad thing was, back in those days, we didn't see very much of her – although when we did, I was always struck by her natural warmth.

There was Charles and Dorothy too, who were natural siblings born into a Jamaican family like me. When their mother could not care for them due to illness, Anne and Cicely took the children in when they were just three and five years old.

Dorothy and I were joined at the hip. We did everything together: shopping, swimming, walking and talking. Anne and Cicely's mother was still alive then and we all called her 'Granny'. She had the most trenchant views and was an old-fashioned Tory to the core. She believed more in 'sending them back' than anybody else I have ever encountered, but when Anne and Cicely would retort, 'What about Charles, Dorothy and Derek?', she would always reply, 'Oh, not them – they can stay.' It amused us no end.

Cicely loved the English countryside and that is where my love of it came from too. We went for hearty walks in 'sensible' shoes with our much-loved dogs. She fell in love with Norfolk and bought a house there, and we spent our weekends and holidays weeding the garden, visiting nearby stately homes and fine-dining on special occasions. We never saw another black face in Norfolk. I can vividly remember the stares when we went to the market town of Fakenham to do our shopping. I knew something wasn't right.

I also remember an early biking holiday in Suffolk. I was staying with the splendidly grand and very clever James Pilkington, from the Pilkington Glass family, and I peeled off from the others to explore more adventurously. Local walkers were amazed to see me: 'How did you get here? We don't see many of your type around here.' Thus I grew up confronted daily by race as seen through the eyes of others.

With that background, I could not help but be interested in

this subject. More than most, I understood what it was to be different – and I always understood, too, that the contribution immigrant communities have made to Britain has been immense.

However, I never would have thought that David Cameron would give me cause to write this book. I have known him for twenty-eight years. I know, perhaps even better, the family he married into, and I introduced the younger David to a good number of political players who would later dominate party and government thinking.

When the time came he lobbied hard for my support in his bid to become party leader. Surprisingly, that was not an easy decision for me as I also had a lot of time for both David Davis, and the popular, but less likely leader, David Willetts. The former was conspicuously consistent on civil and human rights, and, I must say, has continued to be since. The latter has a beautiful soul and is one of the most civilised people I have known; it was a pleasure to properly work with him later. Of course, they all wanted to appear the moderniser, for which my endorsement – fresh from success on *Big Brother* – meant a good deal. Eventually it was to be Cameron whom I supported, publicly and in the numerous private conversations that are at the heart of such campaigns. I believed his promises, although it is a fairly settled question now who was the more authentic moderniser.

It matters no longer. Not since the 'Go Home' ads. I was appalled, truly appalled, by this cynical campaign, designed entirely to stir up controversy in order to maximise free publicity in newspapers. In more than thirty years of active participation in politics, I have never used the 'racist' charge against anyone. I do now. David Cameron's intention in approving that ad was essentially racist. He knows it. We all know it. Few in his own party will say it, but the Conservatives have clearly decided that to win another election they must revert to type. To win, they need to outdo others on immigration and Europe. Out again comes the dog-whistle politics, forgetting again how much good it *didn't* do Michael Howard. And booted out the door of No. 10 went Afro-Caribbean politician Shaun Bailey. He served a purpose – it was crude and it was nasty – but that is how the Tories have always been. They like keeping black people in one place – or in *their* place, as the Tories see it. My history with that party is littered with countless examples of this, and, one day, I shall tell you about those too.

The Prime Minister's modernisation agenda did not last that long, though: what doesn't come from the heart never does. It's no good using words like 'kids', or appearing without a tie in public, and expecting everyone to believe that makes you modern. New suits, or no suits, but the same old mind. That is what we have today and it will not do.

Now, both the Conservative Party and the Labour Party ('British jobs for British workers') are fighting over the same turf. Labour are gently knocking at the same door, as if to say, 'let me in'. They are losing support from their traditional working-class base, and the party advisors attribute this to immigration. I beg to differ. They just don't like *you*, Mr Miliband. It's the oldest trick in the book: blame someone else for your own problems.

Immigration is always getting the blame. The language is always negative. It's all about the problems, the controls, the swamping… The exception to this patter has usually been the Liberal Democrat Party. Impressively, they have resisted the pressure to join in the bashing spree. Indeed, they can be heard reminding people about the benefits to Britain that cultural diversity has brought and how it has enriched our island. They have stood their ground on what is right, which is not always popular, and that is the truer leadership.

And right it is, because the language of demonisation doesn't come anywhere close to the real heart of this matter. The reasons people migrate are many and come from the very roots of the human condition. It's a last option – desperation. It's for refuge – hope, aspiration, inspiration, admiration. It's for protection of family – opportunity, acceptance, recognition, tolerance. They come from fear of torture, in flight from religious fanaticism, in despair of secular despotism; seeking respite from an illiberal world, they just want what others have. They gratefully accept what has usually been freely offered to them. As our emigrant and more successful American cousins know better, migrants migrate for 'life, liberty, and the pursuit of happiness'. They are seldom in it for the laughs. Did anyone ever seriously make this leap in order to claim social security benefits? For that is lately the kernel of the Tory narrative. True, not every dream works out. Not every enterprise succeeds. Things don't go to plan. People need help sometimes, even the best of us. But uprooting everything in order to claim benefits? That phenomenon exists only in the small minds of small men – and the greasy pole-climbing of Theresa May.

No. Migration is driven by freedom from persecution, opportunity and love.

Persecution was the case for the 3,000 Chilean asylum seekers who fled General Pinochet's oppressive regime and arrived in Britain between 1974 and 1979. It was also the case for the influx of people from Eritrea and Somalia in the 1990s. Does everybody know this? Perhaps not, but everyone knows that Somalia is where Olympic gold medallist Mo Farah came from. How many people proud of his elevation of British sport on the international stage can locate Farah's country of origin on a map? When the stadium crowd roared him round the final lap on the final day of the 2012 London Olympics, it was 'Go Mo' not 'Go Home'. When the nation rose to its feet and took to social media, it was not to tweet at Gabby Logan to demand the runner's immediate repatriation. The waving in the streets was not, I think, to helpfully point him to London City airport. He was the best of us then – the positive face of the open and inclusive society that we were so proud to present to the world. Mo Farah's face was a great, British face.

How quickly we forget.

Economic opportunity is another immigrant motivation. The ambition to realise a better standard of living for the immigrant and their family has led Britons to seek warmer economic shores, Australia being an inviting opportunity for many. In the year ending June 2013, 320,000 emigrants departed the UK for greener pastures. So why wouldn't people from other countries seek to take their place? One man's trash is another man's treasure, after all. While some Britons feel they are escaping a sinking ship due to tax hikes and declining services, many from the developing world and poorer EU states view the UK as a land of great opportunity. Kaushik Basu, the World Bank's Chief Economist, observed correctly that migration and remittances offer a vital lifeline for millions and play a major role in an economy's take-off. They enable people to partake in the global economy and create resources for overseas development and growth. Many Middle Eastern, central African and Indian employees remit money home to ensure that relatives in politically unstable territories and impoverished communities are able to meet their basic human needs. It helps them transcend their disadvantaged lives in the longer term.

Strange then that when we speak of our pride in maintaining our overseas aid programme it is usually a reference to spending abroad, despite the fact that inward migration via remittance of earnings is probably our main development aid – and one of the most effective. Mandarins and the quasi-mandarins of the mega NGOs routinely struggle with development aid programmes – how to ensure the money avoids capture by corruption while reaching the people who need it on the ground. Meanwhile, migrant families have long solved that one – they call it Western Union Money Transfer.

Immigration is also about people in love, and we know what happens to them: they get married, poor devils, and, shockingly, seek to live together. Fat chance of anyone stopping that.

The immigration story runs deep through all of our histories, but politicians are weak and have vested interests in a 'them and us' narrative. They like to speak as if immigration is a new thing. It isn't. They encourage people to wish it would go away. It won't.

Many people, oh-so British people, think it is nothing to do with them, but – when they properly trace their own roots – it usually does have a lot to do with them too. In more cases than people care to admit, it's not *whether* they came here, but *when*. In truth, there is no 'them' and there is no 'us'. In truth, we are all in the same boat, and we all eat the same bananas.

It is this one journey, and the history of that journey, that I set out to recount in this book. In reality, the countless individual journeys, from all places, in all centuries, have contributed in many, many ways to making our country great. It is one of the wonderful things about being British that, because we have been immigrants ourselves in so many other places abroad and have enjoyed the unending fruits of trade and empire, we can now tap into the whole world, even while staying at home.

We owe a lot to the empire, which I notice is merely the first of many ideas that we stole from immigrants. We got that idea from the Romans so, before getting to the serious stuff, like most good stories it's best to start with the Romans…

I would have liked the Romans. They came; they saw; they took one look and said: 'Oh no, no, my dears – you're doing it all wrong.' Roman immigration, as I shall call it, changed eve-rything. They sent centurions and stayed for centuries. They profoundly reformed our language. They married. They had ideas and founded institutions. They made the rules (some of them are still our rules). They left us with law. They brought art, architecture, wine, literature, theatre. They dabbled with disruptive and controversial new technology: roads that go somewhere, bridges that connect things, water supplies piped out of the sky … that sort of thing. They thought outside the box. To be fair, they smashed a few boxes and local politicians regarded them as dangerous reformists. But they led the way. Most important of all, they taught the woad-wearing classes a thing or two about looking good – and they liked a nice Bath.

My kind of immigrant, the Romans. And, on that evidence, I am convinced that long before I was Anglo-Indo-Caribbean, I must have been Romano-Nubian also.

They caused much change, those Roman immigrants, but most of it was for the better. It was hugely beneficial, which is why, of course, we still remember it – all of it. But so it has been with a lot of immigration since then, which we don't always remember entirely – and sometimes not at all. Or maybe we choose not to.

That's the story of this book – some counting, but mainly recounting. Of course, the story of immigration is one of chaos. Immigration is not always planned. It's often relentless. It can be appalling – sometimes shocking for all concerned. It has unintended consequences. It's trouble – for those who look for it.

But it's also glorious. It's liberating – for us as well as them. It's been necessary. It's the too-well-hidden secret of a lot of our success. It's the creative fusion within which innovation thrives. It's diversity itself – the guarantee of our future success. Quite frankly, it's amazing. And it's us.

Chapter 2

The fusions that formed the national fabric

OVER MANY CENTURIES, WAVES OF invaders – Romans, Vikings and Normans – have arrived, conquered and settled on the British Isles. In the process, they have defined present-day indigenous ethnicity, cultural mores, religion and language.

It starts at the top. Although apparently British to the bone, our royal family are, in their marrow, the direct descendants of a German bloodline via their eighteenth-century ancestor George Louis, Elector of Hanover, who was crowned King George I in 1714.

Historic French, German or Scandinavian lineages and

surnames are so common as to be regarded as the quintessence of Englishness: Gascoigne, Merson and Scholes are merely the first three I can think of.

And what is true at the palaces remains true all the way to the terraces. The nationally treasured trio of Pauls – Gascoigne, Merson and Scholes – are the quintessence of Englishness too … and of patriotic football prowess. Their surnames are testament to the lineages of historic immigration: French, German and Scandinavian.

The black thread in the Union Jack

Sixteenth-century pay day: the Exchequer roll of 1507 records the first payment to John Blanke, a black trumpeter at the Tudor court.

Nor was it ever just Europeans coming here, but the more diverse historic migrants get written out and forgotten. How many are aware that a black woman, an Iberian Moor named Catalina de Cardones, faithfully served the English Queen, Catherine of Aragon, for twenty-six years as her lady of the bedchamber? And how many Brits were taught about John Blanke during their Tudor history classes? The Afro-Iberian trumpeter regularly performed at the courts of both Henry VII and Henry VIII. In 1511, Blanke had a distinguished role in the Westminster Tournament celebrations, which commemorated the birth of Prince Arthur. The Exchequer roll of November 1507 illustrates John Blanke's pay day; the wage of 20 shillings (£654 in 2014 value) indicates that he probably worked every day of that month.

How many twentieth-century Brits, working alongside Commonwealth citizens in the post-Blitz spirit of reinvigoration, were aware that the African population of London in 1596 was so large that Queen Elizabeth I informed the Lord Mayor of London that 'there are of late divers blackmoores brought into this realme, of which kinde of people there are already here to manie'?

What is more, how many are aware that, while many impoverished northern families sent their sons to work down coal mines during the 1870s, many elite west African families were meanwhile sending their sons to redbrick British universities to study? Sierra Leonean Christian Cole even graduated from Oxford with a Classics degree in 1873.

Another Sierra Leonean, with roots in Nigerian soil, named Dr John Randle, graduated from Edinburgh University as a Bachelor of Medicine and Master of Surgery, going on to be awarded the gold medal in Materia Medica in 1888. He later married Queen Victoria's African goddaughter Victoria Davies – who herself was educated, and excelled, at Cheltenham Ladies' College.

The Kru – west Africans from more humble origins – worked alongside Englishmen as ship labourers and seafarers in port cities including Bristol, Cardiff and Liverpool, thereby greatly contributing to Britain's colonial trade with west Africa. Ships' masters sought to employ the Kru due to what they perceived to be their 'better discipline and greater energy', particularly during tropical voyages.

Diverse Sierra Leone as experiences of empire: Victoria Randle with her children Jack (father of Adekunle Randle – p. 119) and Beatrice.

Hogarth's The Industrious 'Prentice *plate.*

The major waves of immigration did not start in 1945 – there were many previous absorptions into the country: in the late seventeenth century, in the form of the Protestant, and predominately Calvinist, French known as Huguenots; in the nineteenth century, in the form of the famine-stricken Irish; and in the late nineteenth and early twentieth centuries, in the form of the Ashkenazi Jews fleeing persecution in tsarist Russia.

Probably around 50,000 French Huguenots fled to this country following Louis XIV's 1685 move to revoke the Edict of Nantes (which thereby declared Protestantism to be illegal). As a result of this dramatic step, around half a million

French Protestants left the country for more sympathetic havens in (non-Catholic) northern Europe as well as further afield (including South Africa). Many of them crossed the Channel to England, while some made it to Scotland and even Wales. In the years that followed, they recreated a life for themselves based on their weaving skills, which proved much in demand in the booming silk and textiles industries. Spitalfields in the East End of London emerged as a hub of Huguenot activity in the late sixteenth century. A further Huguenot wave reached London in the early 1700s, as the new French immigrants sought to avoid the restrictive regulations applied by the medieval guilds within the parameter boundary of the City of London. This reflected their entrepreneurial acumen, bypassing the incumbents' strategy of placing daunting barriers to new entry. An official government study reported that, in 1687, there were as many as 13,050 Huguenot refugees living in and around Spitalfields and the neighbouring, new, expanding communities of Bethnal Green, Shoreditch, Whitechapel and Mile End. These would be the new towns of the eighteenth century. Persecution overseas had fuelled a boom in British industry and subsequently boosted the British gene pool. It would be interesting to ascertain the percentage of London's historic white English population who have a Huguenot ancestor; the Bow Bells may no longer ring, but the Y chromosomes remain.

Religious persecution was also the driving factor in a later wave of immigration to Britain, namely the influx of Jewish refugees escaping pogroms in Russia and the Baltic states in the late nineteenth century. Britain's Jewish population had finally been awarded full emancipation by Parliament in 1858, albeit this reform was implemented only after decades of interminable wrangling. Benjamin Disraeli became Britain's first Prime Minister of Jewish descent ten years later.

Beginning in the 1880s was an alarming spate of pogroms in what was known as the 'Pale of Settlement' in Russia. Originally created by Catherine the Great in 1791, the Pale extended across what are now present-day Lithuania, Belarus, Poland, Moldova, Ukraine and parts of western Russia. This was the area where Jews were allowed to live – they were prohibited from doing so beyond the Pale. While many of those persecuted set sail for the United States, around 140,000 Jewish refugees moved to Britain prior to the First World War. Most of them set up home in the slums of the East End of London, occupying the rundown homes of the Huguenots. Elsewhere in Britain, many Jewish refugees settled in the rapidly expanding northern cities, notably Manchester, Liverpool and Leeds, as well as the two great Scottish conurbations, Glasgow and Edinburgh.

Many of these refugees had as much to offer Britain as Britain offered them. One such immigrant was named Chaim Weizmann. Originally born in Belarus, the PhD holder – who had previously lectured at Geneva University – found an academic post teaching chemistry to the British students of Manchester University. He was destined to become the first President of Israel.

By the end of the First World War, there were estimated to be around 250,000 Jews living in Britain. In contrast to the experience of many Jewish communities in other countries, such as Poland (many of whom lived in ghettoes), the refugees who flocked to Britain largely assimilated with the local community and went on to distinguish themselves in many cultural and academic fields.

We should be grateful for the misguided politics of persecution in Russia and eastern Europe because it brought so many talented people to this country. Indeed, Jacob Bronowski (Lisa Jardine's father), Sir Isaiah Berlin, Lord Arnold Weinstock, Michael Marks (a founder of Marks & Spencer), Sir Israel Sieff (a chairman of Marks & Spencer), Lord Alan Sugar, Simon Schama, actress Claire Bloom, and writers Stephen Poliakoff and Harold Pinter all have ancestral origins in the Pale of Settlement. The list of Jewish immigrants who have contributed so much to Britain's academic, cultural and business success is a very, very long one.

Or should that read: 'The list of British jobs taken by Jewish immigrants is a very long one'? That sounds like a joke, but it isn't. In a pattern that would repeat itself, the British government – responding to mounting public unrest – began to clamp down on immigration from tsarist Russia with the passing of the Aliens Order in 1905. This followed rising discontent in the

East End of London caused by the influx of Jewish immigrants who were keen to escape oppression and persecution in Russia. Opposition to this recent wave of immigrants centred on the British Brothers' League, a paramilitary organisation formed in 1902 whose catchphrase was 'England for the English'. Sir Oswald Mosley's British Union of Fascists, active in the 1930s, was clearly indebted to this earlier anti-immigration movement.

Irish

Hundreds of thousands of Irish Catholics also crossed the Irish Sea in the nineteenth century following the potato famine in the 1840s. Ireland experienced a massive collapse in the size of its population in the mid-nineteenth century; indeed, it plummeted from a figure of more than 8 million in 1841 to 6.5 million in 1851 as families moved to Britain and the US. It was during this surge in emigration that the Irish working class provided the manpower – in the form of Irish 'navvies' – to build the Victorians' extensive rail network complete with tunnels and stunning bridges such as the viaduct spanning Ribblehead in the windswept Pennines. Their prodigious hard work, along with their ability to consume vast quantities of stout, entered national folklore. It is less well known that around a third of the British Army and Royal Navy were made up of Irishmen.

Ribblehead Viaduct: built by a thousand Irish navvies in the early 1870s in the windswept hills of the Yorkshire Dales.

There was further much-needed Irish immigration during the Second World War and in the post-war years as Britain looked across the globe to meet its needs for willing hands to rebuild the war-ravaged country. It was in the late 1940s and '50s that many Irish people came to settle in towns and cities such as London, Liverpool, Manchester, Birmingham, Glasgow and Luton. Britain offered relatively well-paid jobs whereas Ireland continued to be plagued by slow economic growth and a high level of unemployment. Obviously, such Irish families could never hope to be accepted in Britain, as perhaps could be testified by the writer Edna O'Brien and presenter Terry Wogan.

Here comes Patrick

When an Irish friend of mine was greeted with a '*Dia dhuit*' in the lift on the thirty-second floor of an apartment block in Ankara, Turkey, she was not astonished. The man in the lift had worked for the Turkish embassy in Iraq and had met an Irish nurse who taught him this greeting, which means 'God be with you'. Whether God is with the Irish is anyone's guess but the Irish do turn up in unusual places.

This includes being a significant presence in Britain for several centuries and leaving their mark on many areas of British life.

When current Irish ambassador to Britain, Dan Mulhall, took up his post in September 2013, there were 400,000 Irish passport holders in the UK. From the early seventeenth century, the Irish had arrived as seasonal labourers, and, over time, 10,000 'Molly Malones' – female street hawkers who sold economic goods by day (and some were also reputed to trade more sensual services by night) – were peddling their wares from wheelbarrows around St Giles in the fair city of London. However, these Molly Malones were probably not singing but crying, as being a pedlar was more akin to being a pauper back then. This national group was over-represented at the Old Bailey, particularly for vagrancy offences, with estimates that one-third of the 2,000 beggars in London were Irish at the end of the eighteenth century. Some of these vagrants were forcibly returned to their homeland.

Those who did have houses often lived in squalor. Thomas Beames reported on a house in Saffron Hill having eighty-eight people living in a five-room dwelling, and anecdotes exist of the proverbial keeping of pigs in the parlour. Immigration reached a peak in 1851, after the famine, with 109,000 or 4.5 per cent of Londoners being Irish-born. The push factor after the Great Famine harmonised with the pull factors in terms of demand for Irish labour on Industrial Revolution projects such as canals and then railways. The next wave of post-war migrants continued, and in the 1970s the Irish made up the largest immigrant community in Britain. This generation fared somewhat better, but only just. Limiting long-term illnesses and mental health issues were higher than average; low incomes, low educational attainment, and poor diets and housing characterised this population into the second generation.

But the Mulhall-era passport holders tell a different story. Another wave of immigrants arrived in the 1980s holding degrees and professional qualifications. These passport holders have morphed substantially from vagrant paupers to features on the Rich List, and if they visit the Old Bailey it's more likely to involve tax evasion on their millions. They still occupy traditional niches such as the NHS and the building trade, but the stereotype is shattered. Today, Irish people continue to contribute to all aspects of British public life, but now from a leading position. Patrick is in the media, gives you advice on your investments, optimises the railway system, and utters kind words when you are ill.

The world of fashion

To begin at the top, Philip Treacy has become a leading milliner and dressed royal heads. The headdress that Camilla wore when she married Prince Charles was one such example. Treacy went on to be recommended by Camilla as the official royal wedding hat-maker, with thirty-six heads donning his creations on 29 April 2011. His most famous, or indeed infamous, design is the pretzel fascinator, worn at the royal wedding by Princess Beatrice of York. The controversy centred around whether it was more evocative of a toilet seat than regal elegance. Treacy was even accused of a covert attempt at bringing down the monarchy. This hat only redeemed itself when it fetched £81,100 while being auctioned for charity.

Princess Beatrice's royal wedding hat, courtesy of Philip Treacy.

And it's not just royal heads. He also has loyal clients among celebrities such as Lady Gaga and Sarah Jessica Parker. When Lady Gaga appeared on *Friday Night with Jonathan Ross* in 2010 decked out in a telephone-shaped headpiece with removable handset perched on her head, this notable design had been a collaborative effort between Treacy and Malinda Damgaard. When Sarah Jessica Parker strutted out for both premieres of the *Sex and the City* films, it was with towering and audacious Philip Treacy creations.

Dame Elizabeth Taylor asked him to design a hatpin but he instead offered to show her hats which matched the hatpin. At a meeting to try on various hats at the Dorchester Hotel, he ended up gifting twenty-five to her, considering it a privilege to be able to spend time with her. He has contributed to haute couture collections, including Givenchy, Chanel, Valentino, Ralph Lauren and Donna Karan.

His career spans two decades with his London Fashion Week debut being in 1993 and including an illustrious line-up of supermodels like Naomi Campbell, Yasmin Le Bon, Kate Moss, Stella Tennant and Christy Turlington. Since that initial exposure to the limelight, awards include the title of British Accessory Designer of the Year on five occasions, as well as an honorary OBE (Order of the British Empire) for his exceptional contribution to the British fashion industry.

February 2013 saw the release of a book that features highlights from all stages of his creative process, from the nitty-gritty of the studio to the glamour of the catwalk. A twenty-year collaboration between Treacy and his official photographer, Kevin Davies, enabled access to more than 200 photographs, which allow readers to gain insights into his unique manner of working. This book also includes photos of his most memorable creations including Rosewell (1998), Upside Down Rose (2000) and Fred Astaire Dancing on Discs (2003).

But who is the man behind the hats? Philip Treacy was born outside Galway on the western coast. He crossed over to London in 1988 when he won a place on the MA fashion design course at the Royal College of Art. The following year, one of his hats ended up with leading fashionista and style editor of *Tatler* Isabella Blow. Was it luck that he met his early patron this way? Apparently, people were mistaking her for the Blarney Stone and she was getting kissed way too often, so Philip designed headdresses that kept would-be kissers away. This fashion relationship developed and she even let him set up a workshop in the basement of her home in Belgravia. She wore the flamboyant designs herself and her championing of his work to her friends offered them an alternative to plastic surgery.

And it's not just Philip Treacy with his hats. London Fashion Week showcases catwalk collections from other Irish fashion designers and labels, ranging from the established old hands such as Paul Costelloe and Orla Kiely, to emerging stars like Liam Fahy. Indeed, 2013 offered the biggest number of Irish designers to date the opportunity to present their unique twists to the global fashion industry.

And there's no sign of it waning.

*   *   *

Dublin-born Paul Costelloe has been on the design scene for the last thirty years, moving his designer label base from Dublin to London in 1999. His life took many twists before that move to London. Leaving the prestigious Blackrock College at sixteen, he went to work at a pig factory in Waterford, where, through a process of elimination, fashion design emerged as the path which would use his artistic talents. This realisation took Paul to Paris to train at haute couture boutiques and become a design assistant at Jacques Esterel, and then to Italy as a designer at La Rinascente, a store that had worked with Armani. After his experience within leading European fashion houses, he crossed the pond to join the New York fashion industry on 7th Avenue. On his return to Dublin, he set up his own independent fashion label in 1979 called simply Paul Costelloe Collections.

Costelloe is the most established Irish designer and has been on the line-up for London Fashion Week every season for fifteen years. During those fifteen years, the supermodels associated with his collections have included Jerry Hall, Caprice and Jodie Kidd. More recently, he has transitioned from being merely the opening catwalk show to parading his collection on the final day. Having been the first act for six seasons is testimony to the flair of his creations.

He famously declared in 2009 that his designs have a wide target group, and are for 'international, modern women, aged between twenty-seven and ninety-seven'. Although the age span is broad, locating his flagship store in Knightsbridge in 1994 and placing his range in both House of Fraser and John Lewis does signal the prestige end. Women with a penchant for quality who favour a classic, discreet aesthetic are not the sole target though, as he has broadened to include a new menswear line and designer glasses. Corporate wear is another area where people tend to forget the designer behind it. To his credit, he can list the landmark uniform British Airways used from 1992 to 2004, as well as uniforms for other airlines such as AerLingus, Qatar Airways and Delta Air Lines. Besides airlines, uniforms for British Gas and Sainsbury's supermarkets can be added to those designed for the Orange Arrows Formula One team and the England Women's Cricket Team, who took the crown in both the 2008 Ashes series against Australia and the 2009 Cricket World Cup.

* * *

Another Dublin native who has made big waves in the UK is Orla Kiely. Kiely graduated as a textile designer from the National College of Art and Design in Dublin, and then moved to a New York wallpaper and fabric designer's establishment. Like Philip Treacy, while studying for her master's degree at the Royal College of Art in London, her hat display in the exit show was purchased by Harrods. However, at her father's suggestion she began designing handbags. In the late 1990s, she decided that the laminate cloth used for tablecloths could be used for handbags. She has since moved on from designing handbags to having her designs used on a host of other objects including kitchenware, stationery, furniture, wallpaper and even cars. She has been described by *The Guardian* as the 'Queen of Prints'.

However, Kiely's inspiring lines extend to dresses, and when you are one of the Duchess of Cambridge's favourite labels, there is only one drawback: running out of stock within a day of a royal appearance can be challenging.

The Duchess in a fit-and-flare coatdress for an engagement in Oxford in February 2012.

Kate in a steel-grey dress at the Dulwich Picture Gallery in March 2012.

And it's not only the Duchess, but Carole Middleton also chose a Dancing Girls Tea Dress to visit her first grandchild Prince George in front of the waiting paparazzi.

Entertainment and the media

So the Irish inspire the way you dress, but they are also there to entertain you with music and laughter. That soft Irish accent is ubiquitous in the British media. Names such as Chris Moyles, Ed Byrne, Graham Norton, Dara O'Briain, Paul O'Grady, Paddy McGuinness and Terry Wogan not only sound Irish, but they are either first- or second-generation Irishmen too. Most of their work involves simply talking, but there are also musicians who play a range that extends beyond the traditional Celtic and embraces the classical.

From our waking moments, it was the Irish voice of Terry Wogan – hosting Radio 2's *Wake Up to Wogan* show from 1993 to 2009 and another breakfast show prior to that, from 1972 to 1984 – who, for twenty-seven years, listened to, traded banter with, and generally charmed and relaxed his listening audience, becoming the housewives' favourite. By 2009, he had more than 8 million listeners and they even included the Queen. Wogan was named Best Breakfast Music Presenter at the Sony Awards in 1994. When he stepped down, there was avid interest as to whether the new breakfast show disc jockey Chris Evans would maintain audience figures, although Evans actually beat his predecessor's record by averaging 9.5 million weekly listeners in his first three months in the job.

From the late 1960s, when Limerick-born Terry Wogan flew over from the Dublin-based RTE (the Irish national radio and TV service) to present *Night Extra* on the BBC for two years, this was the beginning of a media legend. In 1969, he took over when Jimmy Young was on holiday and, later that year, Terry was given his own daily show on Radio 1. Then his name was attached to almost every time slot in the radio week. From the aforementioned *Wake Up to Wogan* and *Midday Spin* to *Weekend Wogan* and his short-lived primetime TV show *Terry Wogan's Friday Night,* it sounded and looked like there was no escaping him. The very positive role he played was to have a Wogan effect in helping to lessen the hostility of the British public towards the Irish in the course of the IRA bombing campaigns.

Although his career began in radio, he steadily gained fame and fortune through extending his talent to prime-time BBC television programmes, beginning with *Blankety Blank*, which he presented from 1979 to 1984. He won the Variety Club Award for Radio Personality of the Year in 1974, as well as *TV Times* magazine readers voting him TV Personality of the Year ten times. Extensive television credits would follow: *A Song for Europe, Eurovision Song Contest, Lunchtime with Wogan, Come Dancing, Celebrity Squares,* and his own *Wogan* chat show. Indeed, providing the TV commentary for the annual *Eurovision Song Contest* for more than three decades until 2008 netted him £150,000 per gig towards the end of his stint.

But it is his hosting of *Children in Need* – or, in the Queen's words, 'Terry and the Teddy' – which he claims to be most proud of, having raised more than a quarter of a billion pounds for good causes since the first programme began in 1980. But it was this hosting job that put Sir Terry Wogan at the centre of controversy over claims that he was the only celebrity to be paid for his part in the appeal – and paid the hefty sum of £1,300 an hour. Although he has never denied being paid, he claims to have given his fee to the charity.

When Terry abandoned his banking job in the late 1950s to move into broadcasting, that didn't mean he lost out on the cash. He is rumoured to be worth well over £20 million, mostly thanks to his chatterbox attraction to housewives and all that effortless charm. This broadcasting legend earned £800,000 a year at the radio microphone and £1.2 million a year hosting the Channel 4 quiz show *Wogan's Perfect Recall*; his second autobiography, *Mustn't Grumble* (2006), gained him a £1 million advance; and his smooth Irish tones are also popular with advertisers, including WHSmith, Nescafé and Heinz. Tesco knew that his core audience would be swayed, and are credited with having paid him £250,000 for voice-over work. He received an honorary OBE in 1997, and in 2005 he was knighted as recognition for his services to broadcasting.

* * *

Dara Ó'Briain is a Wicklow-born stand-up comedian and another one of the most recognisable television presenters on

British TV. Described by the *Irish Independent* as 'Britain's favourite Irishman', he is noted for hosting topical panel shows such as *The Panel* and the hugely successful *Mock the Week* since it began in 2005. *The Apprentice: You're Fired* shows him at his best – interviewing Alan Sugar's rejects – and he is also a regular guest on *Have I Got News for You* and *QI*. This multi-faceted graduate in mathematics and theoretical physics began his career on the RTE – like Terry Wogan, but as a children's TV presenter – although he does now present science-related programmes such as *School of Hard Sums*, *Stargazing LIVE* and *Dara O'Briain's Science Club*.

Dara's talents for entertaining stand-up led to him being voted into sixteenth place on Channel 4's *The 100 Greatest Stand-Ups*. This unique combination of science, comedy and irony has won him a place in the hearts of the British public.

* * *

Affable, Dublin-born Graham William Walker – now known as Graham Norton – moved to Britain and tickled the public's comedy spot on the BBC's *Just a Minute* as well as sitting in for Steve Wright and Chris Evans on Radio 2. He carved his own niche after taking over Jonathan Ross's Saturday BBC Radio 2 show in 2010.

After his chat shows *So Graham Norton* and *V Graham Norton* on Channel 4, he went to the States for a while, before moving back to join the BBC and hosting his own comic chat show since 2007 – *The Graham Norton Show* – a one-hour, late-night slot. Presenting the *British Academy Television Awards* and the *Eurovision Dance Contest* are among his other roles, and his talent has been recognised in him winning the BAFTA for Best Entertainment Performance on five occasions. He does not have financial problems either, having sold his own television production company for £17 million, and doing lucrative advertising deals on the side.

*   *   *

A lesser-known entertainer is freelance harpist Jean Kelly, who left her native Cork in 1996 to take up a scholarship to study at the Royal College of Music, London, at the age of eighteen. Her accomplishments include playing at a Windsor Castle reception for the royal family and the Irish President Michael D. Higgins. She was helped by Irish Heritage – a cultural organisation presenting concerts of Anglo-Irish music and other Irish-related events such as poetry readings and literature days – to break the ice with her first professional London concert. Now, as an artistic advisor, she helps to set up concerts and performing opportunities for young Irish musicians recently arrived in London.

However, she does not restrict her performances to the high and mighty: her concerts also reach out to several care homes for elderly Irish people, some with dementia – playing Irish folk songs functions as therapy for them. As she listens to the stories of the tunnellers and other labourers, the hardships and racism they faced in post-war-era in Britain – things she is glad to have avoided – she is aware of owing a huge debt to that generation. Sharing her common musical tradition with them is part of her gratitude and recognition for their forging the way – because of them, she can now integrate into British professional society without losing touch of her Irish traditions and identity. Playing the most requested songs ('When Irish Eyes are Smiling' and 'Molly Malone') to that generation of Irish emigrants – who arrived in London in the 1950s and '60s – compares starkly to the success and wealth stories of the Mulhall-era graduates.

The NHS

When you fall ill, the Irish are very likely to be charged with taking care of you. It's not just the subdued post-Celtic Tiger arrivals who populate wards of British hospitals, Irish accents resounding; immigrant Irish nurses had already gained a firm foothold in hospitals well before the setting-up of the NHS. After its inauguration, 1949 recruitment drives were launched for nurses not just from Ireland, but also from the Caribbean, Malaysia, Mauritius and other far-flung parts of the crumbling empire, thus producing a diverse ethnic mix. Just as with construction workers, lack of job opportunities forced thousands upon thousands to take the boat to Britain to take up roles in the NHS. So many Irish nurses were attracted by

Kakar, Sudhir 467–8
Kant, Immanuel 13, 14, 17
Kaplan, E. Ann 354, 367
Kassan, John F. 359
Kertész, André 334
Kipnis, Laura 632–3, 638
Kluckhohn, Clyde 238
Kogan, Frank 353
Kristeva, Julia 84
Kroeber, A. L. 268

Labour Party 150, 164, 184, 592, 663
Lacan, Jacques 83, 85, 86, 133–4, 325, 466, 489
  'The mirror stage as formative of the function of the I' 133–9
Lacoste-Dujardin, Camille 272
Lafitau, Father 258, 260, 278
Lam, Barnard 234
Langer, Susanne 237
language:
  Chicano Spanish 402–11
  and class distinction 169–70
  denial of legitimacy of 402–11
  and discourse 140
  rhetoricity 465–6, 470, 474, 478
  role of 84, 85
  as sign system 17, 85
  and translation 463–82
  and unconscious 133
  written, as precondition of civilization 105, 106–14, 115
Lawrence, D. H. 524
Leavis, F. R. 149, 154, 557, 663
Leavis, Q. D. 155, 663
Leenhardt, Maurice 268
'legendary psychasthenia' 136
Legge, Gordon 352, 363
Leiris, Michel 271
lesbianism 486–7, 540
  tribal acceptance 391–4
Lévi-Strauss, Claude 105–6, 115, 201, 488, 499
  and culture/nature opposition 83, 84, 299, 500, 502, 511
  and structuralism 199–200
  'A Writing Lesson' 105–14, 116–19, 121–30
Levine, Lawrence 357–8
Lewis, Wyndham 232

libidinal dynamism 134
libido 628–33
Liebling, A. J. 234
Lilburne, John 178
Lincoln, Abraham 48–57
linguistics 117–30, 593–5, 599–600
Lippman, Walter 211
literacy 166–7
  and detribalization 231
  theories 335–7
  working-class 151
  women's 337–50
literary criticism 335, 336
  Afro-American 412, 413, 414, 416–19
  and cultural studies 575, 596
literary techniques, in analysing culture 236, 240–1, 245, 248, 252
literary theories 213, 257, 279, 335–7
literate behavior 334–5
  interpretive community and 337–50
lived cultures 574, 603, 605, 606
Lodge, Thomas 193
Lopez, David I. 278
Lowie, Robert 264, 277, 494, 507
Lukács, Georg 445
Lyotard, François 426

Macaulay, Lord 383, 385
McCabe, Mabel 397
McCarthy, Mary 285
McCombie, Mel 562, 563
Macdonald, Dwight 298
McGough, Roger 191
McLuhan, Marshall 212, 213, 225, 301, 626
  'The Medium is the Message' 225–35
Mailer, Norman 291–2
Majnep, Ian 278
Malinowski, Bronislaw 267
  and ethnographic fieldwork 261, 262, 263, 265, 274
  and Trobriand islanders 258, 260, 262, 263, 274, 488
Mallarmé, Stéphane 89, 92–3
Marcuse, Herbert 82, 210, 211
Marlowe, Christopher 193
Marothy, Janos 363
Marx, Karl 3, 14, 15, 202, 383, 606, 635
  and cultural tradition 179–80, 181
  and Engels 33–4
  The German Ideology 34–6, 181, 200

the working conditions and prospects within British hospitals that, by 1971, it is estimated up to 12 per cent of Britain's nurses were Irish-born.

Today, for staff whose data is available, 11 per cent of those working for the NHS and community health services are not British. Ireland contributes the fourth-highest number of foreign staff to the NHS, outdone only by India and the Philippines and followed by Poland, Nigeria and Zimbabwe. Altogether, 12,600 Irish people work for the NHS, comprising 5,000 of its nurses, midwives or health visiting staff. More than 4,000 UK-registered doctors have also trained in Ireland.

Post-war nurses had to stop working when married, but this profession gave Irish migrant women access to higher-status work than many of their male construction compatriots. A picture of three Irish nurses holding certificates with visible medals pinned on their nursing aprons – they had won the top three places in the 1964 British Nurse of the Year awards – shows the association of excellence with Irish nursing. These prize-winners had trained in Britain under the government's assisted immigration scheme, established in response to NHS labour shortages. Currently, Irish nurses are still being snapped up by the NHS at a rate of about 300 annually. Final-year students get offers before they graduate and they are preferred before British graduates, according to the Irish recruitment agency TTM, contracted to provide the NHS with nurses. Currently, about one-fifth of Irish nursing graduates move to the UK. Why are they so popular with the NHS? Irish nursing graduates have a better standard because of the significant number of placements they undertake during their course. This experience on the ground puts them that one step ahead of British graduates. In any case, despite lower salaries in the UK, lack of jobs in Ireland leaves nurses with no choice but to emigrate.

And what about doctors? In the 1940s and '50s, up to 30 per cent of Irish medical graduates took off, and most ended up in the UK – having English as a first language is a huge asset as they do not face the language barriers of other foreigners. When President Higgins visited London's University College Hospital in April 2014, Irish journalist Niall O'Sullivan interviewed Irish staff – or what he called 'the Irish lifeblood' – who work in Britain's National Health Service (*Irish Post*, 9 April 2014).

Such is the number of Irish personnel that a cockney patient joked: 'You've kidnapped me and moved me to a hospital in Ireland in the middle of the night, haven't you?' This joke had a more serious meaning and more than an element of irony. In fact, it was Ireland that had moved to UCLH, with five of the key clinical figures in charge of this patient being Irish: the speciality consultant, the specialist nurse, the outreach nurse, the intensive care registrar and the consultant in emergency medicine and intensive care medicine. In other words, the whole medical team.

One claim to medical fame came to a Cork-born surgeon, Dr Edward Kiely, who successfully separated Cork-native conjoined twins Hassan and Hussein Benhaffaf – two little boys who were joined chest to pelvis – at another London hospital, Great Ormond Street. But before the birth itself, another Corkman, Pat O'Brien – a consultant obstetrician and gynaecologist who dealt with high-risk pregnancy – helped deliver the babies in December 2009 at University College Hospital, along with two senior Irish nurses, Mae Nugent and Mary Dinan.

This hospital is particularly Irish, with Irish people in all sorts of specialties and roles, from porters and administrative staff, to nurses, laboratory technicians, doctors, and consultants. Eamon Sullivan – the hospital's deputy chief nurse in charge of 700 of the hospital's nurses – is Irish too. Helen O'Toole – lead nurse for pre-registration education – and Josie Gladney – a matron for medical specialties – are two more of the many Irish staff at UCLH. Is there an explanation for the Irish dominance in this profession? One Irish nurse suggests the reason is that the Irish are 'good for the craic'. Having a fun atmosphere certainly lifts the spirit – and is that not part of therapy?

The purpose of the visit from President Higgins was to mark the contribution of Irish people to the National Health Service – the countless Irish staff who work in hospitals throughout the country had their day of recognition. While books have been written and research carried out into those who left Ireland to work in construction, the Irish contribution to British medical care has been given insufficient attention to date.

Business

When the crowds gazed at the Pre-Raphaelite painting by Walter Howell Deverell in the exhibition at the Tate Gallery, they saw *The Irish Vagrants*, a despairing pauper family by the roadside with a half-naked child begging from an indifferent rich lady. This depiction is an example of results of the post-famine influx from the late 1840s as the Irish-born population reached its peak of 602,000 in 1861. The Irish population accounted for about 5 per cent of the population of London and up to 25 per cent of that of Liverpool – it was characterised by poverty, as the more able and enterprising emigrants had chosen America and Australia as their destinations.

Today, both first- and second-generation Irish immigrants number among some of the major British household names.

Who knows? Maybe the descendants of that indifferent lady in the painting are listening to Irish investment advisors in the City. Not only has the City taken on an emerald hue, but over the years – and particularly in the last decade – Irish people have featured prominently in many British businesses, with as many as 50,000 Irish directors currently serving on the boards of British companies.

On the financial front, one of the first notable achievements was the founding of the modern version of the *Financial Times* by the Tipperary-born Brendan Bracken. The non-executive chairman of Goldman Sachs International is Peter Sutherland, a barrister by training, who had already achieved success as Irish

Attorney General and chairman of BP and the LSE. The City UK, a body that promotes the financial and professional services industries in London, puts the figure of workers in those sectors in London at 641,000, of whom about 10,000 in the City – and 25,640 overall – are Irish. Within Morgan Stanley's London office staff of 6,000 in Canary Wharf, an Irish network called Net-Eire has approximately 250 members. The Irish embassy in London relate that about half of the membership of the Global Irish Forum is linked with the financial services sector in London, while the London Irish Business Society (LIBS) networking group say that over one-third of their 1,700 members are employed in the financial sector at every level.

Two notable examples within the banking sector are Patrick Foley and Matt Barrett. Still in his twenties, Kerry-born Patrick Foley can boast a stellar career trajectory. As one of three students chosen from among 900 for the RBS/NatWest graduate programme, he was offered a role at Coutts – the private bank to the royal family – just fourteen months into the programme. Now he provides advice to aristocrats and sports stars on their investments. Matt Barrett, also Kerry-born but passing through Harvard Business School, ran Barclays bank from 1999 to 2006. His large salary and his major restructuring – involving branch closures and staff cuts – attracted widespread criticism. His response to those who bemoaned increased bank charges was blunt: supermarkets do not have aisles marked 'free food'.

Why is the number of Irish professionals in senior

management positions in financial institutions so high? The old negative stereotype of the Irish 'gift of the gab' has morphed into the more respectable 'good interpersonal skills', which can now be monetised. Their reputation for being both hardworking and good with people is key to their success in the financial services industry. Building relationships and rapport with clients makes the key difference, although a competent knowledge base and communication skills are also necessary. Besides working hard, playing hard certainly poses no problem for the Irish either. They have the right package of qualities.

* * *

It's not just investment advice for the aristocrats though. Second-generation Irish, Liverpool-born Terry Leahy served as Tesco's CEO from 1999 to 2011. He began humbly stacking shelves and rose to the top job, where he managed to more than triple profits from £1 billion in 2001, to £3.4 billion in 2010, as well as entering the Chinese market and establishing a presence in thirteen other countries. O2, another household brand name, was headed by Dublin-born Ronan Dunne from 2008, but he is now chairman of Tesco Mobile. This is not a defection, but rather the result of O2/Telefónica's highly successful mobile joint venture with Tesco. In the age of globalisation now, mergers, acquisitions and international partnerships impact upon the business landscape as much as migration, marriages and miscegenation characterise the social fabric.

*   *   *

Both Cork-born Gerry Murphy and Donegal-born Gerry Robinson were CEOs of media enterprises. Murphy headed TV group Carlton Communications until after its takeover by Granada in 2002, when he departed to run Kingfisher, owners of the B&Q chain. Robinson headed Granada, the company which produces *Coronation Street*, among other things. Not only did he include the Blairs among his friends, but his advice was also sought on how to solve national problems. As a TV personality, fronting *Can Gerry Robinson Fix the NHS?* was his main feat. Like Terry Wogan – and despite not fixing the NHS – he was knighted in 2003. Sir Gerry lives with the style of a knight and the dignity expected of his rank. Although, with current property prices being what they are in the Royal Borough of Kensington and Chelsea, he could in fact be said to live like a king. As well as his primary residence in the elite Holland Park, his home in his native Donegal is a Georgian country house replete with a botanical garden featuring a narrow gauge railway, which is open to the public.

*   *   *

The confluence of finance and property – the trademark roar of the Celtic Tiger economy – involved Derek Quinlan, who bought the Savoy Group of luxury hotels in London, paying out £750 million. However, this deal had politically wry moments too. An Irish worker at the Connaught Hotel, part of this group, put the Irish tricolour up the hotel's flagpole. Although it was done without his permission or knowledge, Quinlan cried thinking of his father's role in the Irish army and how this would have been a dream come true for him. Whether or not protocol allows the Irish tricolour to fly above buildings is less of an issue than the metaphorical Irish flags flying in big property deals throughout London. It is said that half of Bond Street is now Irish-owned. Many a professional gentleman may be unaware that the purchase of his suit may contribute to the lining of an Irishman's commercial pocket.

*　　*　　*

The dedicated body for Irish lawyers – London Irish Lawyers Association (LILA) – has a membership of over 800, attracting those from corporate and commercial spheres, to those involved in issues of human rights. Members are at various levels in the field, from freshly minted graduates, to those in more senior posts who are making their mark in British society. Gráinne Mellon, chair of LILA, sees the association's role as helping new arrivals to connect with the Irish legal community in London in order to promote professional and business growth.

The Irish love to get together and so business networking comes naturally. Sinéad Crowley of the Irish International Business Network is highly aware of the significant contribution of Irish entrepreneurs and business professionals to the London corporate world. She has spearheaded initiatives like the IIBN's Future Leaders Programme, which aims to connect proven talent to the next generation seeking to build or develop their own businesses. Jill Tully of the London Irish Business Society, set up in 2009 in response to the influx of Irish professionals to London, has clocked up 3,000 members. These networks all seek to bring together those of the younger generation who have a high level of education, a taste for hard work and an entrepreneurial spirit to meet the leaders who can show them the ropes. These meetings vary from drinks evenings to career and business development workshops. This is something previous generations did not have.

Building and construction

The Irish are almost synonymous with an established expertise in construction at all levels – literally – from deep tunnels to the top of skyscrapers. Within prestigious property development, the Irish builder is there. During the nineteenth and much of the twentieth century, British canals, railways, roads, motorways, the Channel Tunnel and other infrastructures were built with Irish labour and lives. Again, today, within the Crossrail projects, the Irish have been present in large numbers. Such major contractors as J. Murphy & Sons, Laing O'Rourke and Ballymore Properties can easily trace their roots to Ireland. And actual building leads to property development, with Irish developers acquiring brick-and-mortar assets in the City of London and other expensive parts of the metropolis.

The term 'navvy' was coined in the late eighteenth century in Great Britain during the canal construction period, with canals also being known as 'navigations'. Later, the term was applied to describe manual labourers working on any major civil engineering project, and that meant an exponential expansion of the railway system, particularly laying rail tracks and tunnels from 1830 onwards. The requirement for a workforce of 200,000 men building 3,000 miles of new railway line meant that, after the famine, one-third of workers were Irish. These navvies used hand tools: picks, shovels and a wheelbarrow. These tools proved to be more cost-effective than steam-powered mechanical diggers or excavators, which only appeared much later. Working conditions for these railway navvies were infamous, and explosives added to the danger. Irish navvies faced regional hostility for lowering wages, and an industrial dispute involving thousands of navvies spread across the north of England resulting in rioting and murder in the 1860s. These migrant workers lived by the rail line they were building in what would be the equivalent of shanty towns, with huts housing up to twenty men. This hard physical labouring was tempered with heady leisure. Their pay reputedly going on beer and ale and leaving little for food. The philosophy was 'drink and be merry for tomorrow you may die'. The risk of death from collapses and explosions in tunnels was high, with scant regard for safety procedures in the face of a plentiful supply of navvies.

Were the navvies of the great post-war building programmes any better off? The strongest demand for labour came from the West Midlands. In the case of Coventry, which already had a large Irish community, the navvy population doubled in the 1950s as the city needed to be rebuilt from the ruins of the Second World War. Although the demand for labour in the service sectors and skilled labour force also increased, the 200,000 males aged eighteen to twenty-five who arrived between 1951 and 1961 were uneducated Irish emigrants. However, they could offer physical energy and strength for outdoor labour, and that supply matched the enormous demand from Irish contractors.

Many labourers adopted the 'lumper', working casually by day or taking on piecework. This flexible system involved waiting outside Irish pubs and the hiring stands in Cricklewood or Hammersmith every morning from six o'clock to be selected from among thousands of men by gangers. The lucky men were loaded into wagons and taken to the building site.

Some of these Irish navvies rose to wealth and prominence. Some flourished by progressing to subcontracting, then founding their own firm.

One builder, John Murphy, hitch-hiked from County Kerry. He built his business – which undertook large cable-laying contracts – and ended up with eighteen companies in Britain valued at £190 million in 2009 at his time of death. His only trouble was with the Inland Revenue for tax evasion.

The Kennedy brothers, John and Joe, arrived from County Sligo as labourers in the late 1940s. They progressed to subcontracting with different utilities in the public sector. They set up separate companies, the Blue and Green Kennedy firms respectively. John Kennedy Holdings was acquired by Balfour Beatty for £37 million in 2001. In 2012, Balfour Beatty employed around 10,000 employees, who both supported UK customers' needs and contributed a great deal of productivity and tax to the national economy.

Both jubilation and outrage at Irish advancement in the construction industry occurred when Mayo-born Ray O'Rourke completed the purchase of loss-making Laing Construction for £1 in September 2001. This Irishman became the owner of one of the great indigenous British construction companies. Founding his own company in 1978, today Laing O'Rourke is the largest privately owned construction company in the UK, employing over 15,000 people.

Still, today, the Irish tunneller has not disappeared. One person working more on the brain than the brawn side of the tunnel business is Cavan-born Dr Cian Shaffrey. Cian graduated from Cambridge University with a PhD in engineering, having done research on image retrieval. He now leads the Transformation project for London Underground. However, the brawn side does continue. Attractive wages of upwards of £400 per day on London's £14.8 billion Crossrail project are still luring hundreds of Irish construction workers to Britain. When it opens in 2018 – a 21-kilometre section of underground crossing the capital from west to east – it will have been providing employment since 2009.

One thing that has not changed is the link with drink. Donegal publican John McNulty owns and runs the Lucky 7 pub in Cricklewood. Here, Irish construction workers in London meet and the talk about work is interspersed with a few pints. This publican, who is a 'tunnel man' himself, working on the Jubilee line extension in the 1990s, acts as a conduit between companies looking to hire qualified workers and these pub customers. Besides this informal networking system, north London-based John Small runs Cricklewood Construction Training Services, where he uses over twenty years' experience in tunnelling and construction. He estimates that as many as 80 per cent of the Crossrail project's tunnellers are Irish, and claims to have helped up to 400 Irish workers sort out their CVs, qualifications and Construction Skills Certificate Scheme cards within six months.

And is it only a man's world? Angela Brady seems to be the only female in sight. This graduate of Bolton Street Institute of Technology in Dublin is president-elect of the Royal Institute of British Architects. She co-founded Brady Mallalieu Architects, a London firm that specialises in sustainable architecture. She is also a media personality, having fronted *The Home Show* on Channel 4. Britain should perhaps tap in to the economic jolt that has seen businesswomen inject a surge of exceptional dynamism into some of Ireland's top companies. Ireland's largest food group, Glanbia, is run by Siobhan Talbot. Microsoft Ireland and Facebook Ireland are headed by Cathriona Hallahan and Sonia Flynn respectively, while Vodafone's Anne O'Leary became the first native Irish CEO in more than a decade to lead the company. Perhaps the grass is greener on the other side of the Irish Sea for British women of exceptional calibre.

* * *

Some say *'pesce e patate'*; most say 'fish and chips'…

Italian immigrants, mainly from northern Italy, have been a sizeable community in Scotland since the 1890s and one that has invigorated parts of the catering industries. Their acumen in identifying native tastes, wedded with a finely tuned commercial nous, has enabled them to set up scores of successful businesses. These start-ups relied on low initial costs – little more than a range, iron pan and fresh fish purchased daily at local markets – and an awful lot of hard graft. In the twentieth century, the Italian community prospered on the back of serving Scottish natives their favourite supper. Italian enterprise within the fish-and-chip trade and ice cream sector is still resonant in Scottish culinary culture, characterised by family businesses which are now run by the third or fourth generation.

Well-known Scots who hail from this background include Troon-born comedienne Ronni Ancona, Paisley-born actor

Tom Conti, Edinburgh-bred actor Ken Stott, and Largs-born actress Daniela Nardini – a scion of the Nardini ice cream dynasty celebrated for introducing opulent styling and American innovations, including the first ever soda fountain, to the UK.

However, Italy's late entry into the Second World War in 1940 soured the sweet strides many Italians had made in British society. Although most Italians in Scotland were not aligned with Mussolini's politics, they faced persecution via ethnic affiliation. Italian men, including Nardino Nardini, were interned on the Isle of Man, Orkney or Northern Ireland, with deportation to Australia and Canada planned. The deportation plan was overturned by the British government after the *Arandora Star*, a liner transporting 1,200 internees and prisoners of war to Canada, was struck by a torpedo; 486 Italians were killed. As a result, many spent the war years in prison camps within the UK. Yet Italian internees and prisoners of war became a welcome reserve of much-needed help on farms and horticultural businesses up and down the country. There was little antipathy shown to them by the locals.

Britain faced real labour shortages in the immediate postwar period. David Goodhart has estimated that as many as 750,000 people emigrated between 1946 and 1950. To help meet the gap between the demand for labour and its limited supply, the Attlee government adopted a European Voluntary Workers Programme. This enabled former Italian prisoners of war, along with various displaced refugees (notably

Ukrainians), to settle in Britain. As a result, a sizeable number of Italians put down roots in towns such as Bedford – indeed, they provided the labour for the town's brickworks.

In a further move, the Polish Resettlement Act 1947 conferred settlement rights to members of the Polish armed forces who had fought under the British in the war. Around 120,000 Poles took advantage of this offer, rather than gamble on what post-war Poland had to offer. We welcomed them; encouraged them.

In the immediate aftermath of the war, non-white immigrants similarly came to the UK having served in the armed forces or the merchant navy. Having decided to stay, they tended to cluster in seaports such as Liverpool, Bristol, Cardiff and, of course, London.

National gratitude and economic need were confirmed with the passing of the 1948 Nationality Act, which conferred British citizenship on every citizen within the British empire, both from the newly established Commonwealth countries such as India and Pakistan as well as the old dominions. Thirteen years after the statute was passed, half a million people from the New Commonwealth – nearly all of them from the West Indies, Pakistan and India – had put down fresh roots in the 'mother country'. In 1961, 136,000 immigrants from the New Commonwealth entered Britain in search of a new life.

They came because our politicians made it policy to encourage them, and it has remained policy in varying forms ever since. It is plainly true that the scale of movement was unprecedented. But then, as now, it was politicians who opened the doors, made the promises, posted the adverts, laid on the ships ... and it is politicians who have duplici-tously used the people who took up their offers as scapegoats for every grievance since – both real and imagined.

Between 1948 and the mid-1980s, approximately two million people immigrated to Great Britain from Africa, the Car-ibbean, India and Pakistan. The *Windrush* arrivals of 1948 presaged the first major phase of post-war British immigra-tion. The entry of 492 Jamaican citizens marked an exodus from the colonies coinciding with Britain's loosening of the ties of empire.

The Commonwealth migrants entering Britain after the Second World War were British citizens invited to assist in the rebuilding of a nation physically, economically and psy-chologically torn apart by war. The influx of skilled, patriotic and industrious migrants from the Commonwealth enabled Britain to form a welfare state, create the National Health Service, rebuild decimated cityscapes and expand public trans-portation – all vital cornerstones to economic recovery and restoration of public morale.

Caribbean migration was also encouraged by the passing of the McCarran–Walter Act by the US Congress in 1952, which made it far more difficult for people from the Caribbean to gain work and residency in the US. Although the British Parliament passed the Commonwealth Immigrants Act in 1962 – theoretically tightening up the rules – in practice, the

UK government remained amenable to issuing work permits, especially to those Commonwealth citizens who had served in the Second World War. In other words, the government continued to need their service, even while ratcheting up the rhetoric of exclusion.

If it were not for West Indian migrant health workers, would the NHS ever have been possible? Will it continue to exist without more of the same?

The provision of free healthcare for all at the point of use was a noble gesture, but the figures never added up. After sixty-five years, the sums are still askew as there is a world-wide shortage of health workers. 'Britain Needs You' was the clarion call to Commonwealth citizens, particularly young women who could counterbalance the chronic shortage of nurses. In 1955, official nursing recruitment programmes were in force across sixteen British colonies and former colonies. The British government may have welcomed the arrival and subsequent labour of tens of thousands of young women who were trained to staff the NHS, but their welcome by the British people was nowhere near as warm as the temperatures they took or feverish brows they mopped on hospital wards – if, indeed, they were even able to mop them. Immigrant nurses recall English patients who refused their ministrations unless they washed the 'dirt' from their skins. Nurses who back home bathed more frequently than the British weekly bath house custom, had to explain that their skin colour could not be washed off. Facing racism in the 'mother country' that had recruited them to help put the British empire back on its feet was not something the *Windrush* generation of Caribbean migrants had expected to encounter.

Despite this overt racism, significant numbers made the journey. This supply of cheap labour was vitally needed to meet NHS staffing shortages over the following two decades. Dr Peter Carter, head of the Royal College of Nursing, believes that the NHS would not have been feasible without the recruitment of Commonwealth nurses and other health workers. He predicts that, in 2016, once again, the British government will have to fill a predicted employee deficit with overseas recruits.

As it was in the hospitals, so too in the mills. Britain witnessed a surge in immigration from the Indian subcontinent in the late 1950s. This hinged on a major recruitment drive by textiles companies in northern mill towns such as Bradford, Oldham and Blackburn, who were anxious to attract labour to operate a new generation of machinery that was beginning to be installed in the late 1950s in a largely unsuccessful attempt to match international competition and the cost base it enjoyed.

Ted Heath's Tory government pretended to tighten up the rules on immigration with a new act passed by Parliament in 1971. This ended the existing work permit scheme under which many New Commonwealth citizens came to Britain. The act was also skewed in favour of our cousins from the dominions, insofar as it awarded a partial right to those seeking to live in Britain. In other words, if you could demonstrate you had a grandparent born in Britain, you leapt up the queue for a visa. Despite the heightened restrictions, the 1970s saw the National Health Service actively recruiting in Barbados to attract nurses to work in its hospitals, following a similar recruitment practice for doctors on the Indian subcontinent. Meanwhile, London Transport was busy luring men from Barbados to man the buses and tubes.

Over and over they came, wave after wave of political hypocrites, ramping up the rhetoric with one raised fist, but holding out fistfuls of paycheques with the other. Handing out wages to the newly arrived employees they knew to be necessary, beneficial, advertised for, paid for and 'welcomed', but then disparaging them behind their dusky backs. Britain owed these people a debt of gratitude. If immigrants are in any way a problem, the political classes have only themselves to blame and should not be allowed to pretend the migrants themselves are at fault.

By the early 1990s, the number of ethnic minority British totalled four million. But these immigrants mixed and matched. Professional black Britons tended to live in residential communities determined more by class than race boundaries. Half of all British-born Afro-Caribbean men who co-habited did so with white partners; so did a third of British-born Afro-Caribbean women. This was in stark contrast to the US, where only 2 per cent of marriages were between black people and white people.

Who was who in Great Britain: 1991

The results for the 1991 Census question on ethnicity are shown in summary. It recorded the following numbers in Great Britain:

White	51,874,000
Black Caribbean	500,000
Black African	212,000
Black, other	178,000
Indian	840,000
Pakistani	477,000
Bangladeshi	163,000
Chinese	157,000
Other Asian	198,000
Other groups	290,000

Successive surveys published by the Policy Studies Institute[1] testify to the fact that ethnic minority employees worked longer hours, and were more likely to work shifts, than white employees.[2]

From 1983, the Labour Force Survey (LFS) included a question identifying ethnic groups that enabled academic researchers to do some quite detailed analysis of income trends. A rigorous analysis of data for 1988–90 concluded that some ethnic

---

1 The PSI surveys were the only large-scale national studies designed exclusively with the aim of increasing our knowledge about the circumstances of ethnic minorities and how they compare with those of the white population. The first survey was conducted in 1966.

2 Fourth Survey, PSI, p. 348, 1997.

minority groups (Indians, Africans, Asians and Chinese) were in a position broadly similar to, or sometimes better than, white people. By contrast, while some prospered (according to Census findings, Indians and Chinese were over-represented compared to native white Britons, as early as 1991, in professions including academic research and self-employment), many Caribbeans, Pakistanis and Bangladeshis continued to be distinctly disadvantaged.

More recently we have witnessed immigration driven by a global reshuffle following the fall of the Iron Curtain and the demise of the communist empire in Russia and eastern Europe. It is worth remembering that, prior to the deterioration of the Berlin Wall, it was extremely difficult for citizens of Warsaw Pact countries to travel. Indeed, for many East Berliners, the collapse of the wall in 1989 was their first opportunity to set foot in the western part of the city.

Many have pointed out that this massive immigration was the direct responsibility of New Labour. Labour MPs such as Jon Cruddas have noted that, after the landslide election victory of 1997, the Blair administration was keen to underpin labour market flexibility and put downward pressure on wage costs. The Polish plumber was a Blairite success, to the benefit of Britain's expanding bourgeoisie, also fostered by the Blair government. In the New Labour years, Britain saw a total of 3.2 million migrants enter the country, the majority of them from Africa and south Asia, plus a further estimated one million who came as illegal immigrants.

The multicultural framework of modern Britain is woven from diverse strands, with many new ethnic threads entwined into the fabric of society as globalisation rises and international regimes fall. Britain has long been home to migrant groups who are highly visible and relatively well assimilated into towns and cities nationwide via their cuisine, commercial enterprises and cultural expression. Turkish and Greek Cypriots, who fled the 1974 conflict and partition of Cyprus, have established strong and self-reliant communities, particularly in north London. Kurds, who also faced Turkish persecution prior to that (levelled by Saddam Hussein's Iraq), enlisted the support of the London Turkish community to avoid deportation. The number of Iraqi refugees boomed too as a result of the Iran–Iraq War in the 1980s and was followed by another wave during the 1991 Gulf War. Around 82,000 Iranians of diverse backgrounds reside in the UK. Most arrived in Britain after the 1979 Iranian revolution.

Significant New Commonwealth asylum applications on a par with the East African Asian Crisis were made by the Tamils of Sri Lanka in 1985. Ethnic cleansing after the disintegration of the former Yugoslavia created great displacement in the 1990s and resulted in another infusion of culture to Great Britain. Bosnians and Kosovans who were granted temporary protection via resettlement programmes have made the UK their permanent homes. Refugees fleeing wars in Somalia and the Democratic Republic of Congo have stayed on in large numbers – indeed, Congolese refugees have created a substantial community hub in Tottenham comparable with the settling of South American economic migrants and refugees in the London borough of Southwark.

It's not all hardship, though. Economically ascendant migrants from the EU, South America, Far East Asia, west Africa and the Gulf Emirates have contributed to the expansion of luxury goods and service industries and a rapacious rise in London's real estate prices. The charitable contributions of Russian and American migrants of high net worth augment the budgets of many cultural institutions and seats of learning deprived of government funding in times of recession.

What will this mean for Britain's national identity in terms of culture, politics, economics and religious affiliation?

Figures released in November 2010 by the Office for National Statistics demonstrate that, if immigration remains at a long-term rate of around 180,000 a year, the proportion of the white, British-born population will fall from 80 per cent to 59 per cent by 2051. Furthermore, within fifty years the white, British-born community (defined as English-, Welsh-, Scottish- and Irish-born citizens) will fall to less than half of the country's overall population. David Coleman, Professor of Demographics at Oxford University, forecasts that the younger age cohorts of the traditional white British inhabitants are likely to rank as a minority far more quickly since they tend to have fewer children than those immigrants who have arrived since 1945.

David Goodhart, the author of *The British Dream: Successes and Failures of Post-war Immigration,* predicts that, by the time of the next Census in 2021, the 'visible minority population' (including people of mixed ethnic backgrounds) across England and Wales will have risen from 14 per cent to around 20 per cent. Goodhart, who is a member of a highly successful family of Jewish immigrants (numbering a Tory MP and a member of the Bank of England Monetary Policy Committee among its ranks), believes that, 'in the space of less than sixty years', Britain, 'a rather homogenous country at the heart of a multiracial empire', became a 'multiracial country, now without an empire'.

*   *   *

The Latin American countries which once constituted empires for Spain and Portugal now provide the United Kingdom with one of its fastest-growing yet relatively invisible migrant groups. A national taste for salsa to dip our crisps in or to dance to in bars nationwide has been hungrily and rhythmically embraced. So has the transfer of stellar footballers who enrich our biggest teams. But migrants who hail from the continent and the islands that export these flavours, sounds and goal-scorers have yet to fully cross over into the mainstream.

The phenomenon of Latin American migration began in the early 1800s. Politically motivated migrants based themselves in the UK in order to raise funds to overthrow their Spanish and Portuguese colonial masters. The British were happy to assist in weakening the Spanish empire, which was undermining their own imperial interest. Prime Minister William Pitt offered government funds to the Venezuelan political exile Francisco de Miranda to enable him to wage the war of independence, which in turn allowed the revolutionary Simón Bolívar to trump the Spanish monarchy. Bolívar formed Gran Colombia, the first union of independent Hispanic American nations. The state, and Bolivar's vision of South American unity, failed: Gran Colombia's territories are now the countries of Colombia, Venezuela, Ecuador and Panama, as well as portions of Brazil, Guyana and Peru.

A resurgence of Latin American political instability and civil turbulence beginning in the 1970s led to a boom in migrants from the region seeking refuge and asylum in the UK. Notable migrants include the Chileans – mainly academics, businessmen and students – who fled the regime of General Pinochet after his 1973 military coup. Around 3,000 Chileans sought refuge – mainly in the south London borough of Lambeth – between 1974 and 1979. Many more may have settled here too, were it not for Prime Minister Edward Heath's acceptance of Pinochet's government. A small number of Cubans took advantage of the 1960s Freedom Flights sanctioned by Fidel Castro and made their way to the United Kingdom rather than settle in the United States. If more had been able to make it, perhaps the art deco enclaves of Brighton would more closely resemble Miami's South Beach, in temperament if not in temperature.

Other Latin American political migration waves during the final quarter of the twentieth century include those escaping

Argentina's military government, which reigned from 1976 to 1983, and Colombia's narco-terrorism and civil war, fought between left-wing guerrillas and right-wing paramilitary groups during the 1980s and '90s. The UK ranks second as a destination for Bolivian migrants to Europe, perhaps a throwback to our country's popularity to a minority of Bolivians during less politically stable eras.

Latin Americans come in many shades due to the tri-racial foundation of New World societies based on indigenous, Iberian and African lineages. In Latin America, people are identified by their social class *after* they are categorised by the colour of their skin. In Brazil, race is as descriptive as an ice cream parlour menu, with 134 shades from *chocolate, café-com-leite* (coffee with milk) and *morena-cor-de-canela* (cinnamon-hued brunette), to *trigueira* (wheat-coloured), *branca-avermelhada* (peach-white) and *saraúba* (like white meringue). What a delicious mix! Although Latin America has over 67,000,000 more black citizens than North America, you'd be hard-pushed to find a Brazilian or Colombian soap opera that illustrates this fact – which makes one appreciate the Afro-Caribbean characters of *EastEnders'* Albert Square a fraction more.

In the Spanish-speaking nations, most citizens would be classified as *mestizo* – a mixture of indigenous and Spanish lineages – despite the *blanqueamiento* socio-economic and political policies successfully employed by some governments – including Argentina and Cuba – to 'improve the race' by whitening the population. Black soldiers were sent off to war as cannon fodder while European migrants were invited to prosper economically and vanquish the African element of various Latin American societies during the late nineteenth and early twentieth century. Many of the long-limbed and caramel-tanned Latin American models who have migrated to the UK to find recognition, fame and fortune on agency books, city billboards and London buses – or simply obtain work permits to stalk the catwalk during London Fashion Week – are the product of this migration and miscegenation.

Though distinctly recognisable due to a combination of Amerindian, Iberian and African physical features in variant ratios, Latin Americans were unable to tick a bespoke ethnic box during the 2001 and 2011 UK Censuses and thus view themselves as 'invisibles'. The classification as 'white' excludes a rich and variegated ethnic composition and denies cultural recognition, as few would be of 100 per cent Spanish or Portuguese ancestry. Lacking a formal status as an ethnic minority group leaves many Latin American migrants struggling to integrate as both individuals and as a community and many feel under-represented in various social, political and economic spheres of mainstream British society.

Britain's Latin American community is mainly comprised of Brazilians and Colombians, and London's Latin American population is believed to have quadrupled between 2001 and 2011 – at 113,500 it is catching up with the capital's 122,000-strong Polish community. Statistics gleaned from Latin American embassies in the UK suggest a national total of between 700,000 and 1,000,000 migrants. They have an exceptional employment rate of 85 per cent with few in receipt of state benefits – in fact, many workers are overqualified for the jobs they hold. The language barrier and scarce opportunities are often cited as reasons why highly qualified workers fill jobs beneath their capability. A study undertaken by academics at the University of London discovered that 40 per cent of Latin American workers have experienced serious victimisation, exploitation and workplace abuse and they are ten times more likely than the national average to work for below the minimum wage.

Entrepreneurship has proven both a necessity and a gift to many Latin American migrants who have laid solid commercial foundations and built sustainable economic success by catering to the cultural demands of their distinct communities.

Case study: Diana Sach

She has captured the castle

London references were frequently added to William Shakespeare's work. Though set in the Balkans, in *Twelfth Night* he stated that, 'In the south suburbs, at the Elephant, Is best to lodge'. Diana Sach agrees with Shakespeare and, although not chasing the title, she is evidently the queen of the Elephant & Castle Shopping Centre.

Diana arrived from Colombia in 1985. She had aimed to spend a year studying English, but instead spent twelve years working as a sandwich-maker in an Italian coffee shop. Diana picked up entrepreneurship as well as English and, in 1998, opened La Bodeguita, a café delicatessen catering to Southwark's Colombian community. Those yearning for a taste of home or wishing to continue the quality of life they had left behind – but still enjoyed within a strong and transplanted community – could, and still can, sip freshly roasted Colombian coffee, eat super-sweet *postres*, buy frozen yuca fries, purchase borojó pulp (a superfruit whose fame has yet to spread), drink yerba mate (one of South America's most popular green teas), pick up a *molinillo* (with which to froth their hot chocolate), and obtain Salomé shampoo (a legendary hair-loss product the balding men of Belgravia might like to try).

Three successful years later, Diana opened La Bodeguita restaurant. It is also within the shopping centre and serves authentic Colombian food in a lively environment to up to 150 diners. Was it easy to build her hospitality portfolio? 'Authorities and council were very supportive. I learned a lot from them, each part teaching me step by step to know how to settle in a business with all I need at any time.' Confident and successful as an entrepreneur, Diana also 'imports a traditional fire drink from Colombia – Cali Aguardiente Blanco del Valle'. Perhaps in time it will become as popular with London palettes as Polish vodka brands Belvedere and Zubrowka.

A folk etymology once purported that 'Elephant & Castle' was a corruption of *La Infanta de Castilla*, in reference to a series of Spanish princesses including María, the daughter of Philip III of Spain, who was once betrothed to Charles I. Although not correct, the area *is* distinctly Hispanic, centuries after Iberian royalty gave this section of south London some Spanish folkloric flair.

The name of Elephant & Castle is actually derived from what was once a coaching inn. This is, in some ways, rather fitting, as many take the time to stop, rest and refresh themselves at the shopping centre which now proves to be a Colombian oasis in the centre of major traffic junctions. Here, cheques can be cashed even on Sundays and money transferred back to those depending on the income of their relatives to support them over 5,000 miles away. Nails can be manicured at Lonnie's, a dress can be bought from University of Greenwich business graduate Anna Castro, and then tailored – to showcase the curves Colombian women like to display in local nightclubs – at Nicole, a tailor yards away from Anna's store. If they are ever homesick, Colombian music stars often perform London concerts, and Avianca – Colombia's national airline – has an outlet on Kennington Road. A flight to Bogotá leaves four nights a week.

Although the Latin American community in London is almost as big as that of the Poles, its members do appear somewhat invisible. But the Colombian character of London is plain to see, hear, taste and smell within Elephant &

Castle's aged shopping development (although it was the first covered shopping mall in Europe when it opened in 1965, it is now more shabby chic in an era of glass and steel temples of consumption). One could argue that the Colombian community have saved this shopping centre from going the way of many an old-fashioned shopping precinct: redundant, demolished and long forgotten. It has been a very long time since the Elephant & Castle Shopping Centre was known as 'the Piccadilly [Circus] of south London', but you may not have noticed that it has become the *centro comercial* of London's vibrant and hard-working Colombian community for almost two decades. Many Colombians feel as Diana does: 'London is my home; Colombia is a wonderful country I come from.'

*   *   *

My own conclusion is that the current politics is out of step, for the country is already more than multiracial. It is mixed racial. The future is one of fusion, but true integration is increasingly hindered by a politics that pretends to wind the clock back, promising what cannot be delivered, manipulating, heightening and magnifying division mainly for the sake of a one-election political advantage. As we have seen in America, once political activists or political authority – and I have in mind the absurd fringe elements of the Republican tea party (comprising, as it does, loud-mouthed extremists) – become convinced of their own delusional rhetoric of racial purity, it can be very hard to later reposition it in line with reality. Indeed, it becomes the work of a generation to re-establish trust among those new voters who were the target of their political predecessors.

Chapter 3

The West Indian community

THE ANCESTORS OF BRITAIN'S WEST Indian community mostly have one thing in common: they were all slaves. Their forebears were transported to the Caribbean by the British: it proved a very profitable trade.

Slavery was a booming industry in the eighteenth century. The indentured Europeans who were originally used as labour on the fledgling plantations proved ill-suited for the work. They were not used to the heat, and the harsh demands of plantation agriculture resulted in them dying at ten times the death rate recorded in Europe. Most of them shuffled off their mortal coil as a result of malaria and yellow fever. If indigenous 'red-legged' British labour had not been relatively feeble, unable to withstand the tropical climate and fulfil the labour expectations of Britain's plantocracy, the whole immoral business of chattel enslavement might never have been created.

From an annual figure of around 2,000 slaves in the sixteenth century, the Americas' soaring demand for slave labour climbed to more than 80,000 slaves per year at the peak of this trade in the 1780s. Neither the African nor the European population could sustain numbers by natural increase, so the plantation owners opted to import more slaves from Africa. The life expectancy for young immigrants from Europe in the West Indies was between five to ten years. In contrast, Africans had far more resistance to tropical diseases and the rigours of plantation life.

It is recognised today as fact that many of the enslaved were rounded up and sold by Africans themselves. Most of them were war captives, some were criminals, others were political prisoners. Interspersed among this motley crew were kidnap victims as well as relatives sold to pay off debts or for food in times of famine. Yet it is important to acknowledge that they were never viewed as less than human by their African captors. Africans enslaved by Africans could rise from bondage to the throne as was the circumstance of the Igbo Jaja of Opobo. They even married into the families that held them. This would not have been possible in the United States where one drop of black blood marked you as three-fifths human even if you were only one-sixteenth African, or less.

High mortality rates, attributable to a variety of diseases, coupled with low fertility rates contributed to the consistent demand for new slaves in this immoral trade. Demand was directly linked to the rate of economic growth in key commodities, such as sugar cane. It was further underpinned by the belief shared among plantation owners that it would be cheaper to buy a newly imported slave than to raise a slave child from birth on the plantation and wait fourteen years before they were put to work. Later, in the eighteenth century, this gruesome arithmetic began to change; plantation owners even began to give time off for pregnancy and prizes for the number of children women could bear. It is estimated that the real price of slaves rose consistently from about 1680 to the 1840s, increasing fivefold over the course of the century-and-a-half period.

If indentured Britons had withstood the heat and toil instead – and the Caribbean workload had thus been borne by emigrant white English and Irish, not black slave labourers – then perhaps Caribbean migration to Britain now would be as unnoticeable at first glance as that of a Cornishman moving to Chelsea Harbour.

But even enslaved Africans died at twice the rate expected of their age group on their home continent. Plantation agriculture consumed people just as much as it consumed raw materials. However, by around 1805 the enslaved population had become more or less self-sustaining with a large Creole core.

West Indian ancestry is not wholly African-originated and not all West Indians would get away with dreadlocks. It also consists of indigenous – and now mainly nullified – Arawak lineages alongside European, east Asian, Middle Eastern and Chinese heritages, to varying degrees. The Jamaican national motto – 'Out of many, one people' – should relate to the entire Caribbean region.

Some West Indians – mainly from Barbados, Bequia, Grenada and St Vincent – are solely descended from Europeans. These were once the wealthy landowners who made their fortunes in plantation agriculture and international trade, or the 500,000 poverty-stricken Europeans who came to the Caribbean as indentured servants prior to 1840. English aristocrat Lady Colin Campbell was born into one of Jamaica's oligarchic families, a mix of European and Lebanese lineages.

Pioneering trustafarian Chris Blackwell founded Island Records and transmuted British musical culture with the ska sound during the 1960s. Blackwell was born in London, raised in Jamaica and schooled at Harrow; he moves and shakes through the international business world and high society with a truly Jamaican rhythm. Incidentally, Ian Fleming wrote each of the James Bond books within the Jamaican estate Goldeneye, now owned by Blackwell; 007, a quintessentially British cultural icon, has a Jamaican soul as well as a preference for Blue Mountain Coffee.

Many West Indians are directly descended from the Indian and Chinese indentured labourers recruited to replace freed African-descended slaves after abolition in 1833. Indo-Caribbeans – those with ancestral roots in India and the Indian subcontinent – make up the majority population of the former British colony Guyana (actually located within the continent of South America) and constitute a substantial segment of society within Trinidad and Tobago, as well as a large minority in Grenada, Jamaica and St Lucia among other Caribbean islands.

Indo-Guyanese publisher Arif Ali and Professor David Dabydeen have both made a significant impact on British media and academia.

Ali, whose grandparents were indentured labourers, came to England to study in 1957 and went on to build a publishing empire. In the 1980s, he was the proprietor of three weekly newspapers and two monthly magazines employing 140 staff. At its peak, the *Caribbean Times* had a circulation of 28,000 readers. Ali's company, Hansib Publications, today specialises in books covering African, Afro-Caribbean, Indo-Caribbean, Asian and other ethnic minority issues and subjects.

Dabydeen, a successful writer who has added a Caribbean voice to the narrative of English literature, rose from the ranks of lecturer to director. Between 1982 and 1984, Dabydeen worked as a community education officer at the University of Warwick's Centre for Caribbean Studies. He served as president of the Association for the Teaching of Caribbean, African and Asian Literature between 1985 and 1987 and is a professor at Warwick's Centre for British Comparative Cultural Studies. In 1993, Dabydeen was appointed Guyana's ambassador at UNESCO and has been Guyana's ambassador to China since 2010. He is a man of action as well as words.

Pero's Bridge allows pedestrians to cross St Augustine's Reach in Bristol Harbour.

West Indians have a long history of migration to the British Isles predating the arrival of the *Empire Windrush* in 1948 by several centuries. Many Englishmen who owned estates in the West Indies brought their enslaved African chattel to seaports and major cities to work as servants. Bristol, which accumulated most of its wealth from the triangular trade, has a large long-standing post-*Windrush* Jamaican community. The city evokes many reminders of much earlier Caribbean migrants – from Georgian church gravestones to Pero's Bridge which spans Bristol Harbour.

Englishmen with commercial interests within the Caribbean were often born or settled on the islands. Their descendants were able to return to Britain and easily integrate into the population due to their skin colour – they continue to do so today whether as students or naturalised citizens. Of course, it has always been easy for white Caribbean migrants to integrate into Britain's population and society without much notice. Black – and later Asian – Caribbean migrants have faced a much tougher experience, characterised by struggles to find homes, create communities, gain core rights, achieve equal opportunities and get social recognition, as well as resisting racism. Despite these difficulties, West Indian migrants have established a strong black presence in British society and have added multiple brilliant facets to British culture – sport, music, entertainment and fashion – which radiate globally.

Following a Caribbean lead: Madness and other ska bands incorporated elements of Mento and Calypso into their music.

At this point I want to digress into music. This is a big leap but the reality of cultural fusion often expresses itself fastest and most demonstrably in this most fluid of mediums. Blues and then jazz of course conquered the world, but less obvious peculiarities of UK culture include some of the music from the 1970s from white and mixed-race bands such as The Specials and Bad Manners, memorably infused with a Caribbean demeanour and vibrancy.

Madness, the most popular ska band of the 1980s, released 'Embarrassment' in 1980. The song's lyrics plotted the tumultuous effect of band member Lee Thompson's sister carrying the child of a black male. Her familial rejection and the shame that miscegenation brought to her family highlighted a radical shift in British attitudes to race and the rise of mixed-race couplings. It enjoyed twelve weeks in the UK chart. Extraordinary.

It makes me wonder who we should regard as having the more authentic political insight into modern Britain: the election-losing, anti-immigrant Michael Howard, for example, or that other former leader Suggs, the still celebrated singer of Madness? An unfair comparison maybe, and slightly ironic in Michael Howard's personal circumstances, but, for sure, many politicians who play games with the supposed impossibility of racial assimilation simply don't know what is going on around them. They didn't then and they appear to know even less now.

UB40, a mixed ethnic band of Birmingham reggae lovers formed in 1978, is one of the bestselling musical acts in the world, having sold over seventy million records to date.

Entrepreneurship came similarly easily to London-born DJ and music producer Jazzie B, whose parents hail from Antigua. Born Trevor Beresford Romeo in 1963, Jazzie B was a founding member of the band Soul II Soul, which established the evolution of black and British music during the 1980s with the seminal track 'Back to Life'. Jazzie B is known as 'Her Majesty's favourite soul man' since he was awarded an OBE in 2008. His musical excellence has also been rewarded with Grammy awards, the keys to seven US cities and Ivor Novello's first Inspiration Award.

The emergence in the 1990s of jungle music popularised by pirate radio stations was a black British riff on the Jamaican toasting tradition of DJ and MC interplay. Jungle gave way to the 'garage' trend – an organic transmutation of American house music and Jamaican rhythms and rapping styles. Numerous underground artists including So Solid Crew and Ms Dynamite hit the mainstream, winning armfuls of national music awards in the process. This designer-label-heavy subculture and black British swagger affected the style and lingo of British icons, including David and Victoria Beckham. It spawned – perhaps inadvertently – the 'chav' underclass stereotype applicable to poor white Britons, many of whom had grown up in the same social environment, sharing the cultural norms and lingua franca of the younger generation of working-class West Indians.

Britain is justifiably renowned for its music around the world, but it's not just the Beatles and the London Symphony

Orchestra. Music, perhaps more than any other aspect of culture, thrives on diversity.

Fiery impact: north Londoner Niomi Arleen McLean-Daley aka Ms Dynamite exploded into the mainstream with an original mix of British and Caribbean musical genres.

New Commonwealth migration to the UK for people born in the Caribbean: 1891–1961

1891	8,689
1901	8,680
1911	9,189
1921	9,054
1931	8,585
1941	No Census taken
1951	15,301
1961	171,800

Source: *Passage to Britain*, Walvin (Penguin Books, 1984). The 1963 Home Office Report used Census data from listed years.

Most Caribbean contributions to British culture are widely believed to stem from the Afro-Caribbean Britons who can trace their roots to the *Windrush* generation. Yet it is not often remembered that, prior to the major wave of Caribbean migration necessitated by the Second World War, West Indians entered Britain as merchant seamen, entertainers, artisans, labourers, soldiers, sailors, students and businessmen among a host of other roles. Significantly, the majority of these migrants were male. The *Windrush* wave of immigrants from the Caribbean settled mainly in poorer run-down parts of London and the south east. Then, as now, there were striking differences in individual inner London boroughs. Wandsworth and Lambeth, for example, are characterised by relatively high black-to-white ratios, while others, such as Newham and Southwark, are much lower.

As there were few long-established Caribbean communities when the *Windrush* arrived in port, most settlers married local white women. Over the subsequent generations, their descendants were counted as indigenous white Britons. Black Caribbean Britons form the majority of mixed relationships in this country, recorded at approximately 680,000 in the 2011 UK Census. Furthermore, in its 2012 report, 'The Melting Pot Generation', the think tank British Future found 'around a third of black Caribbean men and a quarter of black Caribbean women had a partner from a different ethnic group'.

The 2011 Census revealed that Britain's mixed-heritage population had doubled to 1.2 million in one decade. The face and attitudes of Britain are certainly changing.

Perceptions of immigration are coloured by the fact that ethnicity is not always discernible at first glance. Atomic Kitten singer Natasha Hamilton and deceased reality TV star Jade Goody – once globally denounced as a racist – both have mixed-race fathers. This nuanced picture is further underpinned by the boom in fake tan and the British predilection for sun beds. Is this really just sun worship, or is there also an unconscious sea change in people's view of beauty? This point may seem churlish to the reader, but the context should make clear why this is a serious point. In the 1960s and '70s, some Britons were obsessive about racial identity, even racial purity. The thing that was thought to be superior was the white Anglo-Saxon race. The sun wasn't for the British, and people covered up. This was long before cheap flights to sunny destinations, which the British working classes liberally adopted. The scene in *Shirley Valentine* comes to mind, when she decides to leave the monotony of her terraced home in search of the Greek sun. She detests her own kinsman abroad for their rowdy behaviour and dislike of the local cuisine.

Immigrants are not different from natives in any crucial sense or in any way that matters. I have no idea what people mean when they talk of 'British values'. I do know what they mean, though, when they object to aeroplanes being blown out of the sky in the name of Allah. I know what they mean when they talk about duty, and respect for the law. These are values that transcend national boundaries. We didn't invent these values and it's time that we stopped behaving as if we did.

Case study: Edward Johnston

The man with the Midas touch

Edward Johnston was born and raised in Kingston, Jamaica, until the age of eight, when political instability forced his family to migrate. 'Jamaica became politically unstable because of Michael Manley's friendship with Fidel Castro. We weren't allowed to have or move US dollars, so bank accounts were being frozen and it was quite a scary time. Everybody thought we were going to go communist.'

Many prosperous Jamaican families fled the island for

Canada, the US and the UK; the Johnstons left Jamaica in 1975 and lived in the Bahamas for one year and then Miami for five, before returning to Jamaica when the Jamaican Labour Party government came into power and the family patriarch could request their return for commercial reasons.

Johnston is the great-grandson of Charles Edward Johnston, the enterprising banana-grower who, in 1929, formed the Jamaica Banana Producers (JBP), a co-operative that empowered Jamaican growers to successfully compete with the exploitative United Fruit Company. The organisation went on to become a publically listed company, vertically integrated from plantations to supermarket shelves. JBP was a powerful player within the export industry until exiting the market in 2007 during the international trade banana war.

Johnston decided to follow the path of his paternal line, rather than the medical background of his maternal family: 'I did think about which direction I was going to go in. I was always my father's son and felt proud to be a fourth generation working in the Johnston business.' He returned to Florida to gain a BA in agricultural management. In 1992, he acquired a UK student visa and went on to complete a post-graduate degree in shipping from the University of Cardiff, before joining JBP's London office as a shipping manager. Johnston has been based in the capital since 1992, when he fell in love with the city and a Spanish national. After marrying, he became a naturalised EU citizen and permanent UK resident – a status he could also have gained via his employment status. 'I moved to Miami for a year and a half in 1994 to experiment, to see if I could stand Miami life; I didn't like it, so moved back to London and haven't left since then.'

In 1998, Johnston began an MBA at City University underwritten by JBP. A fateful encounter with a lacklustre Jamaican patty inspired the business plan required as part of the course. It in turn became the blueprint for Johnston's successful company Jamaican Patties Ltd, whose flagship brand Port Royal patties is now a market leader. The brand is sold across the UK in the leading supermarkets Asda, Tesco, Morrisons and Sainsbury's, as well as via Ocado, and wholesale to the catering industry.

Sowing the seeds of success

Despite his impressive business background, Johnston faced the same hurdles less-established Caribbean entrepreneurs encounter when engaging with UK financial institutions: 'I was able to get a personal loan of £25,000 which I had to guarantee myself.' He was also tenacious enough to secure two commercial investors in Jamaica and a DTI grant of £25,000, equivalent to 20 per cent of his investment in plant equipment. The pressure Johnston faced was intense: 'It was nerve-racking, at one point we were burning £12,000 per month. We broke even in the second year. We achieved that magic number between a good sale price and the volume of sales.'

Dubbed 'the WICKEDEST patties in the world', Port Royal

patties give an authentic taste of home to the UK's Jamaican migrant community and match the superior quality British tourists have experienced during Jamaican holidays. Despite supermarket buyers agreeing that Port Royal had the best-tasting patties at the time, it did not always translate into contracts. Achieving industry accreditation and finding favour with the Leyton branch of Asda – which then championed the products to be stocked in twelve other stores – allowed a breakthrough that led to the brand being stocked in over 100 Tesco branches and other shops.

Supermarkets are notoriously tough in negotiating contracts and squeezing supplier margins, pitting competitors against each other in a survival-of-the-shrewdest strategy whereby the ultimate winner is the store's profit and loss account. Johnston says: 'We are always looking at ways to reduce our costs without reducing our quality. Everybody is going through the same thing.'

Port Royal launched a premium line of patties for wholesale to higher-end restaurants and has many other gourmet diversifications in development. Exports to Germany, Sweden and Switzerland foretell expansion success throughout the European market in the longer term.

* * *

In recounting the contribution made by West Indians to the British way of life, it is striking to see the way in which so many Afro-Caribbeans have been erased from the history books. This habit has probably contributed to the marginalisation of black people across the country – yet it was not always the case.

Black Caribbean men were so well established as sailors that, by the nineteenth century, they were known as 'Black Jacks' throughout Britain. This was an unknown piece of our history for the generations of British children who chewed the eponymous and ubiquitous liquorice sweet.

While most British schoolchildren since the Victorian era would have recognised the name and likeness of Crimean War nurse Florence Nightingale, it was only in the twenty-first century that they were made aware of her Jamaican rival – 'doctoress' Mary Seacole – who, with remarkable self-assurance, administered Creole medicines and instinctive kindness and saved many lives. Her sepia tone would be the perfect match for a £10 note.

The West India Regiment has served Britain for over two centuries.

During the First World War, 15,000 Caribbean immigrants were recruited to the British West India Regiment, and a portion worked in munitions factories in the north west of England. Others served Britain as sailors and soldiers, just as their enslaved and free ancestors had done since the 1790s. King George V disagreed with Secretary of State for War Lord Kitchener's view that black British soldiers should be barred from joining the forces. As a result of the King's intervention, 15,600 West Indians – two-thirds of them Jamaican[3] – made up the dozen West India Regiment battalions which saw service across several theatres of conflict. In practice, these troops were assigned dangerous tasks rather than allowed to fight head to head. Perhaps this reflected the notion that it was unthinkable for black men to kill white men, even if they were the enemy?

Accordingly, they loaded ammunition, dug trenches and lay telephones wires in dire conditions. Sadly, when peace was restored, their contributions were overlooked and the black presence became unwelcome: Caribbean migrants felt the full force of the race riots that swept British cities in 1919.

In 2012, journalist, activist and film-maker Marc Wadsworth produced the elucidative documentary *Divided by Race, United in War and Peace* to honour the Second World War contribution of his late father George 'Busha' Rowe, his elderly uncle Laurent Phillpott and the numerous other fellow West Indian

---

3 The remaining third were drawn from the Bahamas, Barbados, British Guiana (now Guyana), British Honduras (now Belize), Grenada, the Leeward Islands, St Lucia, St Vincent and Trinidad and Tobago.

servicemen. Their involvement in the Second World War effort was largely overlooked by the majority of history books. The multi-generational production featured young media students and elderly veterans on opposite sides of the camera. Marc Wadsworth estimates that over 16,000 West Indian volunteers defended Britain from the Nazis in this crucial time of danger. Those in the merchant navy participated in dangerous convoys to ensure supply routes at sea remained open. The risks they took are reflected in the 5,000 deaths recorded as a result of German U-boat attacks.

Some 6,000 Caribbean volunteers served with the RAF; the majority of them – 5,536 – on the ground and 300 as aircrew. Jamaica's national newspaper, the *Daily Gleaner*, created a 'Bomber for Britain' fund that enabled colonies and dominions to donate money to the war effort. By 1941, enough money was raised to purchase twelve Blenheim planes. In recognition of this immense contribution, Lord Beaverbrook – the wartime Minister of Aircraft Production – renamed the No. 139 Squadron the No. 139 (Jamaica) Squadron so that, in his own words, 'Jamaica's name shall evermore be linked with a squadron of the Royal Air Force'.

Eighty West Indian women joined the WAAF (Women's Auxiliary Air Force) and thirty volunteered for the Auxiliary Territorial Services. Patriotic British subjects from the Caribbean received a warm welcome from Britons as both people and fellow comrades; they lived with them in cities nationwide and died with them on many battlefields. But just as had occurred in the First World War, good relations soon soured after the enemies' defeat. Despite protecting the motherland from Hitler, West Indian service personnel soon realised that her bosom was no longer as warm as her welcome. 'When will they go back home?' was a question raised by many indigenous British citizens. The response was a shock to those who had risked their lives, known any of the 236 killed or missing in action, or seen the 265 injured. Many Caribbean patriots had grown up singing the 'Eton Boating Song' in the tropical breeze at their Anglican schools. They looked up to the British monarchy and flew the British flag, so volunteering for the war effort was seen as their honourable duty as colonial subjects. For some, it had also been a matter of racial pride to fight Hitler, a man who described black people as on a par with anthropoid monkeys. Yet, sadly, after fighting for British liberty, West Indian service personnel encountered racism – the very social scourge they had fought to vanquish.

* * *

The God-fearing folk who arrived in Britain from the West Indies in the late 1940s had been raised with the ideology that Britain was their 'mother country' and that they were citizens of a global network connecting them to the rest of the world. Regardless of whether they viewed the British empire as a great institution or an oppressive coloniser, Britannia played a core role in – and greatly shaped – the lives of its Caribbean colonial subjects. In return, West Indians would soon play a core role in putting the 'Great' back into Britain and in shaping the lives of those within the British Isles.

London Transport: a major employer for West Indian immigrants.

The post-war terrain and government called out for West Indian labour, actively recruiting and subsidising female nurses, for the newly introduced health service, and fit men, to work for London Transport. The 492 Jamaican *Windrush* arrivals of 1948 formed Britain's first major phase of post-war immigration. As British citizens, Commonwealth migrants were invited to assist in rebuilding a Britain devastated by war. This was a nation with a bruised morale, battered by bombs and in dire need of human capital.

The Windrush: *the first liner to bring immigrants from the Caribbean to post-war Britain.*

Arrivals on deck of the Windrush.

On the whole, Caribbean migrants were optimistic and perceived that their new home would bring them a raft of opportunities. Most of the passengers on the *Windrush* paid the hefty £85 fare for ship cabins usually shared with six other travellers. For many, this proved to be an ominous preparation for their new life in Britain. Faced with notices warning 'no blacks, no dogs, no Irish' they were obliged to acclimatise quickly to sharing rooms with other migrants. What doesn't lynch you makes you stronger: racial discrimination in the housing market necessitated West Indians clubbing together to buy their own freehold properties. Ironically, this was the foundation of an asset base that has bolstered many families right up to the present day.

Further Jamaican ships followed the *Windrush*, including the SS *Orbita* and the SS *Reina del Pacifico*. A record number of 1,100 passengers were aboard the SS *Auriga*, which left Kingston on 2 August 1955. The SS *Castle Verde* followed suit, with a full ship of passengers, within days. Vessels from various countries entered this new business and plied the route between the Caribbean islands and Britain.

Most Caribbean migrants did not follow in the footsteps of Dick Whittington: very few believed the streets were paved with gold but it was a shock to their tropical constitutions to experience streets glazed with ice and snow. Indeed, second-hand overcoats were brisk business in the Caribbean of the 1950s, and sharp-suited arrivals put the locals' sartorial standards to shame. On arrival, West Indian migrants were largely disappointed, if not alarmed, by their reception from the natives.

While some residents were consistently kind to the new immigrants, many others – both working-class white citizens and their social superiors – were quite the opposite. The former were a conservative bunch, tied to an all-too-familiar diet of poor food, soulless music and drab clothing that rarely strayed from a uniform range of grey. Their cultural tastes tended to match their attire. The latter had better resources and a welcoming minority of them were heirs to the same mentality as the cosmopolitan 'Bright Young Things' who had embraced black entertainment culture during the 1920s in elite London clubs and private houses. Some scions of the upper classes, albeit not all, delighted in the vibrant revelry of Calypso music and the sensual opportunities the West Indians brought to drab London. Dr Stephen Ward of Profumo fame was one of them.

By and large, the locals were less godly than the new arrivals, but they had no qualms barring the newcomers from their churches. The fact that many ex-servicemen from the West Indies felt obliged to set up their own branches of the Anglican Church and the British Legion speaks volumes for the degree of assimilation in those pioneering days – and even more on how far the nation has come in terms of race relations since.

The Notting Hill area once known as 'The Piggeries', and now one of Britain's most exclusive enclaves, was a bedrock for arriving West Indian migrants who served as cash cows to notorious landlords such as Peter Rachman. These landlords used to 'sweat' their property portfolio assets by installing prostitutes in the flats and encouraging them to work night and day, or by letting the flats out to Caribbean immigrants. Adopting this approach to his rapidly growing real estate empire, Peter Rachman was able to collect £10,000 a year in rent from a house which only cost him £1,500 to buy. By 1959, it came as no surprise to learn that he owned eighty houses in the Notting Hill neighbourhood of the capital.

However, it is worth pointing out that the Caribbean community did not necessarily loathe Rachman, although he charged them £6 to rent a flat, when a statutory-controlled English tenant was only paying £1 a week for a similar place. Rachman could be patient with black tenants who fell into arrears – perhaps he felt an affinity with fellow marginalised outsiders. It may surprise some readers to learn that a West Indian social worker told Rachman's biographer in the 1970s: 'He was a swinging guy. He liked us, and we liked him.'[4] Oppression sometimes breeds a surprising understanding between minorities: Rachman may have exploited West Indian migrants – to the extent that his legacy is immortalised in the economic term 'Rachmanism' – but he allowed the migrants the basic human right of shelter, which in turn afforded them a base and foundations from where they could navigate their new lives in a frequently turbulent society.

Notting Hill's West Indian community added carnal scandal as well as carnival spice to swinging 1960s London. The

---

4 Quoted in *An English Affair: Sex, Class and Power in the Age of Profumo* by Richard Davenport-Hines, published by Harper Press, 2013, p. 181.

notorious affair that brought down Secretary of State for War John Profumo was sparked by a gunshot from Johnny Edgecombe, an Antiguan ex-merchant seaman who was jealous about what his lover was getting up to in her new-found life in high society. Edgecombe and Profumo, poles apart in terms of social status and background, shared the same lover – Christine Keeler.

Society's shock and disgust at the interracial affair is now viewed as anachronistic, not least because Britain's mixed-race population is the fastest-growing UK ethnic group, comprising 1.2 million citizens in 2011. But in 1963, it was a different story: strong opposition to mixed relationships mirrored British social values.

Most of the first Caribbean migrants were men – some single, others married. Once those with dependants had established themselves and acquired the means to sustain the families they had left behind, they sent for their wives and children. The succour and camaraderie provided by family members would have provided solace from the racist stereotyping, active discrimination and more subtle institutionalised prejudice they faced in the workplace and some social contexts.

The post-war boom meant Englishmen were loath to work in poor conditions for long hours on low pay. Indigenous British women had become more selective when choosing their careers due to the freedom they found during the war years. As a result they often preferred secretarial and clerical appointments over nursing jobs. The number of single female

West Indian migrants increased from the 1950s in response to a recruitment scheme devised by the Ministries of Health and Labour, in synergy with the Colonial Office, the General Nursing Council (GNC) and the Royal College of Nursing, to engage colonial nurses.

Caribbean women borrowed money and found sponsors in order to fund their fares, repaying these loans with their wages over time. In line with the plans of the GNC, the Colonial Office and colonial governors, the women had envisaged training for three years, gaining two years' invaluable work experience, and then taking up nursing positions in the Caribbean. In sum, relieving Britain's staff shortage was a means to a greater end. Yet, as things turned out, most of the Caribbean nursing positions were taken up by expatriate British women.

Caribbean women were mainly placed as resident trainees in psychiatric hospitals treating post-war trauma patients; they also filled shortages in hospitals for the disabled, elderly and chronically sick. The women were disappointed at the Britain they encountered: the stories they had heard and the impressions they had built up since their Caribbean childhoods were proven to be no more than fairy tales and myths. After completing basic two-year State Enrolled Nurse (SEN) training courses, the majority of black nurses found they could not graduate to the higher level State Registered Nurse (SRN) course or receive a promotion.

As West Indian nurses held the requisite British passports until 1962, they received indefinite leave to remain in Britain.

As the SEN qualification was not recognised in the West Indies, many made the most of nursing opportunities in Britain, no matter how limited. Others overcame the obstacle to working in general hospitals by switching to midwifery, a profession they excelled at and grew to dominate.

Caribbean migration trends were also encouraged by the passing of the McCarran–Walter Act by the US Congress in 1952, which made it far more difficult for people from the Caribbean to gain work and residency in the US. Instead, they increasingly looked for work 5,000 miles away – hence, the surge in emigration to Great Britain between 1955 and 1962.

The growing colonial independence movement and the threat of British immigration legislation underlined the need for prospective migrants to leave sooner, lest later not be possible. Caribbean citizens were accustomed to travelling abroad to find suitable work and proved highly adaptable to new nations and labour markets. Since the abolition of slavery in 1834, British West Indians – from nations including Barbados and Jamaica – had travelled to secure land and work in less-populated British territories and non-British Caribbean and American nations such as Trinidad, Costa Rica and Panama. Over 100,000 migrated to work on the Panama Canal and many more settled in Canada and the US to pursue education, employment and land purchase.

Journalist Donald Hinds claims that, by 1955, 18,000 Jamaicans had emigrated to Britain – 'equal to the entire population of Bridgetown, the capital of Barbados'. Data does show that

27,550 Caribbean migrants entered Britain in 1955. The entry rose to 49,650 in 1960, and 66,300 by 1961. In 1962, the British Parliament passed the Commonwealth Immigrants Act, which tightened up the rules, and restricted free migration from the Commonwealth and colonies to all except students, visitors and dependants of those already in the UK.

If your passport had not been issued in Britain or you were not a registered citizen of the UK and colonies, labour vouchers issued by the Ministry of Labour were a pre-requisite to entry. Vouchers were categorised in three bands: the first for those with a definite job offer; the second for migrants with certain beneficial skills or professional qualifications; and the third were generally issued in order of application, although ex-Second World War service personnel were prioritised. The Commonwealth Immigrants Act allowed for colonial subjects to be deported for the first time.

The act achieved the desired effect: in 1962, Caribbean migrant entries decreased to 31,800. The following year, only 3,241 Caribbean migrants entered Britain. After a peak of 14,848 was reached in 1965, Caribbean migrant numbers fell significantly to under 10,000 entries in an average year.

British West Indian migrants to Britain came from a wide variety of backgrounds, ranging from highly qualified professionals to unskilled labourers, yet all shared the common characteristic of industriousness and adventurousness – they wished to work and they were open to new ways of living, despite the struggles they were sure to face.

Case study: La Beba

Her life is what she made it

An exceptional example of the British Dream, which many sought but never realised, is Zurich-resident and former model, La Beba. She was born Norma Gibson-Thompson, shortly after the Second World War, in Barbados's parish of Saint Philip – a countryside idyll on the island's easternmost end.

After the Second World War, her parents were wooed by the visit of Winston Churchill and 'grabbed the opportunity' advertised in local newspapers to come and assist the rebuilding of Britain. They soon left the Caribbean and settled in Croydon. 'They came as hospital workers, then my sister came at eighteen and studied nursing. They left me with my granddad.' Norma's face lights up at the mention of her grandfather in much the same way as it would later be illuminated by some great fashion photographers.

When Norma was thirteen and a half, her parents had saved enough money to send for her – a common practice within West Indian migrant families at the time. Children were often left behind with relatives while a foundation was laid by hard-working parents who wished to welcome their offspring into a stable home life on a par with that left behind. The extended family structure was, of course, physically fragmented, but families found strength in unity and worked hard to stay together in Britain and keep in touch with those back home. Dressed in her Sunday best, Norma took a 22-hour British Airways flight – stopping off in the US – and arrived in the 'freezing' United Kingdom, which in time she acclimatised to. Her lifestyle changed significantly in the UK: when her parents went out to work and left her at home, they did not continue the schooling that the artistic and intelligent teenager had thrived upon in Barbados.

One day, fate took over her education from where her grandfather had left off. Norma spotted an advert for the London Academy of Modelling on Old Bond Street. 'I went to Lucy Clayton first – the gentleman, he wasn't sure. He said, "We can train you exactly, but we cannot guarantee you jobs."' There was a slim niche for black models back then, no matter how graceful their poise, long their legs or elegant their carriage. 'When I was going down the stairs, he called me back. He said, "I'm gonna take you." I said, "No thank you, I don't take second chances."' Norma never has looked back. Confidence, the cornerstone laid by her grandfather, has taken her far: 'I went over that same day to the London Academy; the next week or so they told me how much. I paid, trained there and, from that moment, my life has changed.'

Norma soon signed with the renowned Black Boys Model Agency. Her first job was in Sweden and she stayed there for over two years before going on to have a successful modelling career, living *la dolce vita* at the height of Italian society. 'I never had this racism thing. There's something about how my grandfather trained me that people saw this – the *qualities* – so I was accepted everywhere.' Norma's confidence, forthrightness and positive life philosophies have allowed her to mentor many young people who lack confidence, direction and equal opportunities due to social and economic marginalisation.

Norma's staunch family foundation, high self-esteem and cultural pride combined with her great emotional strength and tactical outlook served her well in decades and locales where reactions to immigrants were, at times, hostile. For many then, as now, migration amounted to survival of the fittest.

Norma's contemporary, the Nigerian model and actress Minah Ogbenyealu Bird, fell from grace selling raunchy kiss 'n' tell stories that were decades ahead of the trend on today's Sunday tabloid front pages. Minah's descent was slow and fuelled by various social factors. She died a recluse in local authority housing in 1995, her body lying unfound for weeks. Norma is pained and compassionate in remembrance of the socialite who was 'like a sister' to her: 'For a black person in those days, she had the whole of London.' But as Norma knows – and instils in her young mentees alongside the maintenance of high personal standards, cultural esteem and social etiquette – life is what we make of it and should be lived as a straight path bordered by confidence and discipline. 'That foundation has to be prepared by the parents, but unfortunately, sometimes, it is not, for a variety of social reasons and personal circumstances unique to the individual experience of life.'

The lessons Norma has taught to a lucky corps of young black adults in Europe and the Caribbean will hopefully be learned by many more in the future. She hopes to positively affect their lives via her future educational and media enterprises, which will be disseminated – and should resonate – much further and wider, to those most in need of good frameworks to ensure the building of successful lives. Norma charitably dedicates her life and resources to serving as a role model for, and assisting the positive development of, younger black generations. She laments of her own youth: 'If I had the knowledge of now [as a youth], I could have been in Parliament.'

*   *   *

A sign that immigrants from the Caribbean had finally been accepted came in 1987 when, at the general election, three black MPs were returned to the House of Commons. They were Bernie Grant in Tottenham, Diane Abbott in Hackney and Paul Boateng in Brent. Paul Boateng went on to become a Cabinet minister in the Labour government. He was joined in May 2003 by Baroness Amos; the Guyana-born peer was the first black woman in the Cabinet, appointed Secretary of State for International Development.

Chapter 4

The African community

'THERE AIN'T NO BLACK IN the Union Jack' and 'Go back to where you came from' are two of the more polite jibes thrown at people of African origin living in Britain. Indeed, the owner of a Vietnamese restaurant on London's Kingsland Road was forced to apologise to a Ugandan-born diner in June 2014, when a Vietnamese waiter told her to 'Go back to your own country'. But many indigenous Britons are as ignorant as new British migrants when it comes to the length and depth of the African presence on the British Isles.

Whether directly descended from immigrants hailing from the continent of Africa or, alternatively, having arrived via the triangular slave trade, it is remarkable to note just how long

Africans have exerted an influence here in Britain. It is worth remembering that Africans, as we know them, were the first people to live on earth. Fossil evidence and genetic analysis illustrates the evolution of modern humans from the original *Homo sapiens* living on the continent of Africa 200,000 years ago. It is now said that Africans may have begun to step out of the continent as long as 125,000 years ago. These pioneers adapted to the climatic and geographical terrain of their new homelands across the globe to become the faces we now recognise as the characteristic hallmarks of the world's ethnic identities.

Roman Britain: ruled by Africans

Septimius Severus, the founder of an African dynasty of Roman emperors, ruled England between 193 and 211 AD. The contemporary chronicler Cassius Dio commented that 'Severus was careful of everything that he desired to accomplish'. Among his manifold achievements were: the restoration of peace after a succession of tumultuous conflicts in the late second century; the reinforcement of Hadrian's Wall; and the legislation enabling marriage for those in military service.

Severus managed to maintain his African eating habits by ensuring his favourite foods were imported to his kitchens from Africa. Likewise, Roman Africans on the British Isles were adept at retaining the high standard of living they had enjoyed back home.

In 1901, the skeleton of one of fourth-century Roman York's grandest ladies was found within a stone sarcophagus. She was an African woman who lived the high society life of her times. Among the luxuries buried with her were two bracelets: one carved from elephant ivory, the other of Yorkshire jet, along with a perfume flacon of blue glass. Genetic testing in 2010 identified this woman as a black African in robust health who was raised in warmer climes but who died of natural causes when she was between the ages of eighteen and twenty-three. She may have been a Christian as she was buried with a bone carved with the Latin words '*Sor ave vivas in Deo*' (Hail, sister, may you live in God). The residents of the London borough of Southwark – which the University of Roehampton has established is home to 'the greatest concentration of African Christian churches anywhere outside the continent itself' – would surely exclaim 'Hallelujah!'

'Multicultural Britain is not just a phenomenon of more modern times,' says Hella Eckhardt, a senior archaeology lecturer at Reading University. The common view that African immigrants to the British Isles prior to the twentieth century would always have been enslaved or burdened by perceptions of low status and living in port towns is entirely erroneous. Eckhardt points out: 'We're looking at a population mix which is much closer to contemporary Britain than previous historians had suspected. In the case of York, the Roman population may have had more diverse origins than the city has now.'

No doubt to the surprise of many, if one digs down beneath the surface of some English family heritages, one is likely to find a diversity of ethnic ancestries, stemming back to Roman times. For instance, the Africans who came to live here on behalf of imperial Rome freely intermarried with the local population. A 2007 study by Leicester University unveiled the fact that seven Yorkshire men with a rare regional surname were carriers of a genetic signature only found in west African-originated males. The ancient hgA1 Y chromosome is extremely scarce even within its region of origin, which encompasses Mali, Senegal and Guinea-Bissau. Eeh, by gum.

*   *   *

More recently, Africans were strongly ensconced within the courts of many British rulers, centuries before their forced labour filled royal treasuries. The Scots appear to have been particularly fond of courtiers from the African continent. One such individual was Elen Moore – one of two African women captured from a Portuguese ship – who was baptised and absorbed into the Scottish court as a favourite of Margaret Tudor, Queen of Scots. Elen was honoured with an extravagant tournament in June 1507. The accounts of King James IV of Scotland detail expenses for African servants, musicians, guests and 'blak ladies', lavished with sartorial luxuries including satin gowns, slippers and ribbons as well as occasional cash gifts. The 1505/6 accounts of the Lord High Treasurer of Scotland include living expenses for the King's black drummer. He lived at the royal palace with his wife and child, and the King paid no less than 28 shillings to the nurse who brought along the drummer's baby to be presented at court.

South of the border, Cumbria proved to be more of a honey pot in ancient times for migrants of African descent than it is in modern Britain. This could have been more from necessity than choice, though, as African soldiers made up a large segment of the Hadrian's Wall garrison. Other Africans no doubt engaged in the trade and services required to sustain Roman life and operations during the centuries of occupation. Meanwhile, in neighbouring Yorkshire in 1687, John Moore – listed as 'blacke' – purchased the freedom of the City of York. This elite honour granted Moore the right to bear arms, graze his animals on York meadows, and fish in the city's rivers. In this respect, John Moore bears the distinction of being the only black person on the York rolls.

Portrait of Elizabeth Risby with African pageboy, circa 1670.

Peregrine Bertie, Lord Willoughby d'Eresby (1555–1601) with African servant.

The presence of Africans is beginning to be uncovered on free-men's rolls in a number of other English cities. Like a rose called by many names, during past eras Africans retained a distinct identity regardless of the many terms used to describe them including Blackamoores, Blacks, Moors, Neygers, Nigers, Negroes and Ethiopians.

The surname Moore, with which many early British Africans appear to have been christened, could be derived from 'Moor' – a historic term for indigenous Africans – or the masculine Latin forename 'Maurus' – which denoted dark skin. Shakespeare's Othello was of course a Blackamoor general, who had distinguished himself in the service of the Republic of Venice.

Tipping the balance

The Elizabethan era marked a change in royal attitudes to African visitors to the British Isles, particularly if their presence was not temporary. In this period, it was not uncommon to walk through the streets of London and encounter a variety of ethnicities and a mosaic of skin tones, in much the same way as one would today. Although in smaller numbers, an African presence was as ubiquitous on the streets of London as within the works of William Shakespeare. African migrants were not as plentiful in Elizabethan Clerkenwell as they are in today's Peckham; however, they managed to carve out a distinct niche for themselves. Lucy Negro, for example, was a dancer at the Virgin Queen's court, and later went on to be a successful madam of a famed Clerkenwell bawdy house – she is reputed to be the model for the 'Dark Lady' of the Bard's sonnets. Contemporary accounts tell us that Lucy was known to cater for 'ingraunts' (immigrants) as well as the country's aristocracy. A heady mix.

It seems that Tudor Britons were both apathetic and intrigued by the African population. Their presence was not a new phenomenon and their positions in court or within local industries were not unusual. Hundreds of Africans – perhaps more – worked in the entertainment, domestic and manufacturing sectors. This is reflected in church records. For example, Domingo – 'a black neigro servaunt unto Sir William Winter' – and Suzanna Peavis – 'a blackamore servant to John Deppinois' – are both listed within the parish records of St Botolph's, Aldgate, in the City of London.

Africans lived alongside the indigenous English, and they married them, too. As far as English common law was concerned, they were free to do as they pleased, so long as it were legal; as far as early Tudor England was concerned, slavery was an institution of the future.

Enslavement

The change in relations came about in around 1600, just prior to the time when James VI of Scotland assumed the English throne as King James I. Britain's black population increased as many African servants and galley slaves on Spanish ships – captured for their precious cargo – were freed. This was liberation Elizabethan style.

Contemporary documents reveal that: 'The Queen is discontented at the great numbers of "negars and blackamoores" which are crept into the realm since the troubles between Her Highness and the King of Spain, and are fostered here to the annoyance of her own people.' The remedial strategy of transporting the Africans to the Barbary Coast of north Africa may be the first incidence of government repatriation. Pressure was placed on English merchants trading with the region to pay for the Africans' accommodation and sustenance until Elizabeth I's ships could take them back to the African continent. It is unclear whether Her Majesty's wish was granted, but it is apparent that her edict did not extend to established black citizens or immigrants whose presence had nothing to do with the Spanish conflict.

Queen Elizabeth I's greatest dreams of wealth were realised via the capture, trade and toil of Africans enslaved as a direct result of her sponsorship of Plymouth slave trader John Hawkins (a cousin of Sir Francis Drake). Although Londoner John Lok is the first recorded Englishman to have traded African slaves – he brought five men from Ghana to Britain in July 1555 'in addition to the usual cargo of elephants' teeth and palm oil' – Hawkins pioneered the triangular trade, profiteering at each port of call.

Queen Elizabeth's rental of the 700-tonne ship, the *Jesus of Lubeck* (originally purchased by King Henry VIII), allowed Hawkins to undertake a longer voyage in which he transported 400 to 500 Sierra Leonean captives. This single voyage generated a 60 per cent return on his investment. The vast profit would have enabled the Virgin Queen to encrust her opulent dresses with yet more pearls, which incidentally were harvested by Africans brutally enslaved in Spanish crown colonies. Queen Elizabeth had permitted Hawkins to transport Africans to the New World 'with their own free consent'. He agreed to this stipulation, but his coat of arms, bearing an African bound in chains, is testament to his disregard for contractual terms and human life. Queen Elizabeth was outraged by Hawkins's enslavement enterprise and mused: 'If the negroes were carried off by force it would be detestable and call down the vengeance of heaven upon the undertakers.' However, her growing awareness of the vast profits to be generated from slavery, along with the surety of a state funeral, soon overrode her spiritual anxiety. It would certainly be interesting to know more about how her 'lytle Blackamore' – lavished in 1577 with a 'Garcon coate of white Taffeta, cut and lined with tincel, striped down with gold and silver' – came to work for her. In 1607, the colony of Virginia – named in Queen Elizabeth's chaste honour – became the first permanent English settlement in North America. The colony's – and, by extension, Britain's – wealth and power were oiled with the blood, sweat and tears of enslaved Africans. The commercial trade in Africans was brutal and inhumane, but it represented a major source of income for merchants throughout the British empire for another two centuries.

In 1772, there was a landmark case in the English courts which outlawed what was referred to as chattel slavery. In *Somerset v. Stewart* (98 ER 499), Lord Chief Justice Mansfield ruled that English law did not support the institution of chattel slavery and so an enslaved African named James Stewart – who had been purchased by his British master Charles Stewart in a British crown colony in North America, with a view to selling him to a plantation in Jamaica – was breaking the law of the land. The judge ruled that: 'It is so odious, that nothing can be suffered to support it, but positive law.' Significantly, Lord Mansfield's own great-niece, Dido Elizabeth Belle Lindsay, was the daughter of an enslaved African woman. He had raised her at his own home, the stately Kenwood House in Hampstead, and made sure to confirm her freedom in his will of 1793. Furthermore, he bequeathed her £500 outright and an annuity of

£100 – a large amount of money in those days. Sadly, Dido's last known direct descendent, Harold Davinier, died in 1975 living under South Africa's apartheid regime, where he was classified under the race laws as a 'white man'.

In the eighteenth century, many Africans in Britain were actively engaged in the abolition movement. Several of them had their own personal stories published, including: the testimonies of freed-man Ignatius Sancho (who arrived in England in 1731), former slave Ottabah Cugoano in 1752, and self-emancipated Olaudah Equiano in 1767. Their first-hand recollections and powerful prose greatly influenced public opinion and assisted the abolitionist cause.

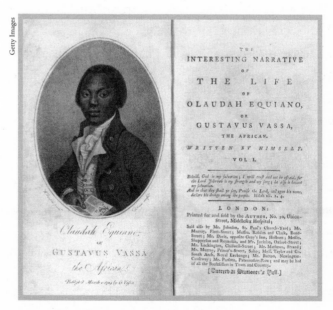

Olaudah Equiano.

African migrants in Britain during the 1800s occupied a wide and diverse range of roles in society – much the same as most Englishmen of the time. The west African Kru – skilled seafarers and ship labourers from Liberia and Sierra Leone – contributed greatly to Britain's colonial trade in west Africa, following the abolition of slavery. Gold Coast trader William Hutton noted in 1816: 'The Kru people are remarkably industrious … They speak English, and are happy to be employed as labourers, sailors or in any other capacity.' As seamen, the Kru were a normal sight in British port cities, as they waited between ships or settled down after securing shore work. They inhabited a limbo of race and class: in west Africa they were relatively well-off working-class citizens; in England they occupied the bottom of the working-class hierarchy due to the colour of their skin. A 1910 parliamentary inquiry found, for example, that 'approximately three in five distressed black people were seamen'.

After the First World War, many in the Kru community were demobilised and had to contend with a labour market in steep economic decline. Liverpool, in particular, had a surfeit of sailors, so many Liverpool-based Kru seamen migrated to south Wales in search of better wages and opportunities.

Yet 1919 was a year characterised by race riots in several port cities, including Cardiff, Newport, Glasgow, Hull, Liverpool, London and Salford – the final destination of the Manchester Ship Canal. The cause for this conflict was a belief shared by many white workers that their black counterparts provided cheap labour and therefore 'stole' jobs that should belong to indigenous Britons. This hostility was underpinned by a misconceived view that black people had risked less during the war. In the ensuing riots, some Africans and West Indians lost their lives, while Arab, Chinese and south Asian sailors were also assaulted. This is a sad yet forgotten episode in British history.

In a further distressing initiative, the National Union of Seamen (NUS) launched a high-pressure campaign against black seamen throughout the 1920s. Under the 1920 Aliens Order, Africans with British nationality were classified as 'aliens' if they could not produce paperwork to verify their status when disembarking from ships. As seamen did not have to carry passports, and their discharge certificates were not permitted as proof of nationality, African seamen were in a precarious position.

In Cardiff, even those with correct papers were classed as aliens and harassed to repatriate to their home countries. Professor Laura Tabili appraises the 1925 Aliens Order – which registered 8,301 black seamen nationwide between 1925 and 1927 – as 'the first instance of state-sanctioned race discrimination inside Britain to come to widespread notice'. The presence of the Kru is still discernible in many port cities: the mixed-race populations of Liverpool and Cardiff are as British as the dulcet vocals of Dame Shirley Bassey.

On the one hand, Africans at the lower end of the social

strata struggled with class and race barriers within the British labour market and general community, including racial segregation and rampant discrimination. On the other hand, Africans who claimed elite provenance enjoyed levels of access to the upper echelons of society which most Englishmen and women of the era could not even contemplate. Indeed, when the December 2013 edition of society magazine *Tatler* trumpeted 'The Nigerians have arrived', the editorial was, unfortunately, around 150 years too late. The upper classes of Nigerian society have sat proudly at the top table since the Victorian age, and the emergence of the commercially powerful and socially ascendant 'African Victorians' – many of whom were the first black people to study at Britain's most prestigious universities in the nineteenth century – set a powerful economic trend.

As mentioned in Chapter 2, Queen Victoria's African goddaughter, Victoria Davies, was a pupil at Cheltenham Ladies' College between 1881 and 1883. The daughter of the wealthy Yoruba merchant James Pinson Labulo Davies, she went on to marry the Nigerian surgeon and political pioneer Dr John Randle, who was educated at Edinburgh University. Their grandson, Adekunle Randle, served as a British Crown Prosecutor until his retirement in 2013, when he resettled in Lagos, Nigeria. His son Bayo was called to the Bar of England and Wales in 2012, putting stock to the African adage: 'If you know his father and grandfather, don't worry about his son.'

Case study: Adekunle Randle

A law unto himself

Adekunle Randle arrived in the UK from Nigeria in December 1988. 'I got married. My wife happened to be British and wanted to come back and do her tertiary education here. I didn't mind to come along for the adventure.' He was just twenty-six years old and a newly qualified barrister. He intended to work in England for just a year or two to gain experience then 'leg it back to Nigeria'. He resettled in Lagos in 2013 to set up a practice of his own.

During the colonial era – and still to this day – many Nigerian barristers, including ninety-year-old Adedapo Adeniran (the oldest living old boy of Lagos's elite King's College secondary school), studied law in Britain and were called to the Bar at Lincoln's Inn. 'The received English legal system is a large body of the law that is practised in Nigeria,' Adekunle notes. He is aware of the colonial legacy of British rule in west Africa and the reason many Nigerians continue to study law at British universities and post-graduate legal institutions.

In his clipped and precise English, which bears the patina of decades spent prosecuting criminals at the Bar yet retains a distinctive Yoruba accord, Adekunle recalls: 'When I first came to England, I spoke with a very thick Nigerian accent. I was conscious of it so I made sure I took steps to address issues of elocution.' He took formal elocution classes of his own volition and at his own expense, and found that they optimised his relations with legal peers and his delivery in court.

He was asked to recall any incidents of racism directed against him while working within the British legal system:

> The one that strikes me the most: when I re-qualified after being a case worker and was posted to the same team, some of the white lawyers there actually protested that it was inappropriate for me to [go from] assisting them to then being their equal. They found that quite uncomfortable. When the meeting was heard, I was not at that meeting. But I heard it was quite heated.

Six months after his promotion to lawyer, a colleague asked him if he knew there was a lot of controversy surrounding his appointment and then advised him to raise the issue with his line manager. Adekunle's line manager admitted it was true and that there had been no need to tell him about the racism that could have potentially sabotaged his legal career:

> He put it in a very nice way: 'Ade, I must be frank with you. You are the first black person in this team as a lawyer and it was raised.' He was meant to make a representation to personnel to stop my posting there. He confessed he did call personnel but it was too late. Because I had already been posted, they couldn't do anything.

Social scientists describe racism as a system that, as an institutional arrangement, is maintained via policies, practices and procedures which deprive people of opportunities and experiences due to their racial identities. Institutionalised racism is defined as a system of inequality that denies people the benefits, opportunities and rewards to which they are entitled, in social areas including education, employment, finance and housing, on the basis of their race. Where social scientists and commentators observe racism as a social weapon, I believe it is a shot in the financial foot, as, in practice, it prevents minority professionals reaching the apex of their innate potential and developing successful careers that would add value to British industries, the economy and wider society. Although, if Adekunle's line manager had gotten through to personnel before he was posted to his team, perhaps his life story would have been one of struggle instead of success:

> I knew I had to be twice as good. Every time I went into court I made sure I mastered the facts and had an impeccable grasp of the law. There may have been some areas I might not have anticipated but, because I prepared well, the rest of my confidence would see me through.

Indeed, Adekunle's line manager told him that, prior to his posting, he came to court to clandestinely observe him practising. He admitted that Adekunle performed well above expectation – in fact, just as well as some of the established lawyers. He told him that he had 'confounded the doubters and none of them could raise it because you excelled'.

Among black lawyers, Adekunle's line manager had a tough reputation. He was observed to never pass black lawyers at their first probation. Yet when it was time for promotion, this line manager gave Adekunle 'one of the best reports he had ever given anybody, black or white'.

Adekunle – this Yoruba forename is translated as 'royalty fills the home' – puts his successful legal career down to the foundation his Nigerian background and family heritage provided. His grandfather Dr John Randle was a great pan-Africanist and social radical who fought for Nigerian colonial surgeons, such as himself, to be paid wages equal to their white colleagues in the 1890s. Alongside fellow Nigerian Dr Obadiah Johnson, Randle won equal pay and other benefits for himself and his fellow African medics. This confidence in the face of discrimination was obviously inherited by Adekunle.

Of the issues he encountered at work he says 'I did not allow this to affect me. I didn't see that as my portion. I did not let other people's problem become my problem. I refused to take their problem.' Confidence is surely king. Having a thick skin, impenetrable psyche and tenacious resolve is the armour necessary to ensure minority professionals are fit to survive in the economic jungle until the day the social system of white supremacy – the operationalised form of racism in the West – is effectively dismantled.

Among the British professional classes, Nigerians are at the forefront of the African segment of the BME demographic. They tend to successfully transplant their clout in west Africa to the British Isles with consummate ease, dynamic panache and upward mobility. 'I think there is something about Nigerians,' says Adekunle. Their confidence is socially ingrained back home and often reinforced via an expatriate community whose meeting grounds include the church, the dance floor, and restaurant or class tables. This confidence is often mistaken as arrogance by other African and Afro-Caribbean migrant groups – although some are truly arrogant.

Adekunle is a down-to-earth man who treats everyone he meets with the respect he would expect for himself. 'I wasn't conscious of being superior to anyone. I was just being me.' His principles of fairness and justice, combined with a natural confidence, made him a man who would not fit into, what some might prejudge to be, his 'place'. He also had no qualms about fighting his corner against attempts to undermine or bully him. In his first year, a stand-off with a judge who ignored his applications led to him making a formal complaint to the Director of Public Prosecutions (DPP). The outcome favoured Adekunle, who simply said, 'nobody should push you', and, in the long run, he earned the respect of that judge. It is clear that directly challenging racism or bullying of any sort in any area of life is the only way to permanently and successfully resolve either matter.

The divide-and-rule tactic employed by Britain during the

empire – and accurately remarked upon by Diane Abbott in a 2012 tweet – is alive, kicking and marshalled by some black people themselves in contemporary society. Adekunle says that he 'was aware of the racial divide and the tension between the various groups. Between blacks and whites and blacks and blacks as well.'

Prior to working with the CPS, Adekunle worked with Lambeth Council as a registration officer during the period in which the Community Charge was introduced. In conversation, a co-worker of Jamaican extraction referred to Africans 'selling off their best people' during the transatlantic slave trade:

> There was that discrimination between Jamaicans and Africans, particularly Nigerians. I don't know whether she thought I was acting superior to her, but there was nothing like that at the back of my mind. That was my perception over time, that she thought I was better than her, but I didn't think that.

Over time he found out this was not an isolated incident.

> Other friends of Nigerian extraction related their experiences from Jamaican sisters and brothers. But over time I think it was a lot easier for me to get past that because there was no guilt on my part and I did not feel antagonistic towards her. The best I could do was be friendly to her and exchange ideas but she was not really receptive.

The reluctance and inability of some segments within minority groups – or even groups as a whole – to work together among themselves, in practice of communal support or group economics, prevents them from realising their full potential in British society. If the National Association for the Advancement of Colored People can report that a black dollar only circulates within the African-American community for six hours – compared to one month in the Asian-American community – and that, out of $1.1 trillion buying power, only 2 cents of each dollar spent by African-Americans are in black-owned businesses, then the UK figure must be quite depressing.

When Adekunle joined the Crown Prosecution Service, 'there were very few black lawyers'. In contrast, black people were over-represented within the ranks of support staff, ushers, clerks, administrators and the like. 'You might find more Asian lawyers, but in terms of the Africans and Afro-Caribbeans, very few.' He noted there were more Africans than Afro-Caribbeans and that the Afro-Caribbean cohort tended to be female and practise in areas such as housing and immigration. In quality, Jamaican-born barrister Courtenay Griffiths makes up for the lower quantity of Afro-Caribbean males at the Bar. In 2011, he was shortlisted as Crime Silk of the Year in the influential Chambers UK Bar Awards.

On why some black children and young adults find it hard to reach their full potential at school or in their careers, Adekunle observed that it may be due to the difference between family structures and networks in the UK:

You will educate your brother's children [pay their school fees] and your brother would educate your children; there is the extended family that took care of you and you don't put your parents in any home either. The family network in the African context is very strong. Parents tend to accumulate wealth to ensure the future of their children. There is the attitude that, 'When I'm gone, I must leave something behind for my children.'

Adekunle's father Jack Randle, who died when he was fifteen, left behind a vast estate of landed property. His father before him had done the same. Adekunle says his father's legacy 'will one day be inherited by the next generation'.

It is not easy for most African migrants to continue or reach the standard of living they may have enjoyed or been able to attain back home in the UK. Not every man is blessed with a father who will leave him a portfolio of assets back in their country of origin. Only a minority of men are able to produce the capital required to build such a portfolio in the land of their settlement. Although many black boys have excellent fathers who provide for their needs and help them achieve their wants, it seems too many are cursed with having absent ones who invest nothing in the formation of their characters.

When it comes to who is the liability in this equation, it appears that, without the correct emotional investment and life guidance, fatherless boys can grow up to be liabilities to their very selves.

It is evident that Adekunle's children are his wealth, as a Yoruba proverb extols: 'Parents would sell their houses to educate their children; your parents would go hungry.' Although both of his great-grandfathers – Thomas Randle and James Pinson Labulo Davies – were wealthy pioneering businessmen who left behind great legacies, Adekunle provided for his children via his own earnings. His younger son Damilola is studying a mechanical engineering degree at Loughborough University. His eldest son Bayo has followed in his footsteps although in civil practice, so appears for either plaintiffs or defendants. Adekunle appraised his son's rise to the Bar in comparison to the many black boys of African or Afro-Caribbean extraction who find themselves on the wrong side of the law:

> Before he started school at all, I was sending him for debating classes, prose and poetry and drama classes. He was very, very good at it. He had excessive energy and that was how I coped with that. If I had a different mind-set I could have beaten him up, but instead of that I saw the opportunity, the potential: catch him young, he has got this energy and could go in this direction.

As a crown prosecutor, Adekunle faced the outcome of what can happen if black boys are not caught young and nurtured within the bosom of a family and wider community, who can instil sound values and promote positive socialisation. He found that many of the black males in the dock had no support, relative to many white males. At the youth court he observed: 'Parents or some guardian were often required to come to court but there were times we had to delay proceedings or they did not even turn up at all. It would usually be someone from social services who would then come and stand in.'

As well as giving support to his sons, Adekunle rates the education system for aiding the development of their characters and careers. Bayo attended a good state primary in a London suburb, a private secondary, then gained a first-class honours degree at Nottingham; ranking third in the year. He then trained for the Bar at Kaplan Law School before completing his master's at Corpus Christi College, Oxford.

Adekunle also believes that progressive peer groups are important: 'The group he [Bayo] moved in were all of the same mind-set – aiming to be doctors, lawyers, engineers.' It is easy to see how many can fall through the cracks of society or fall victim to fatal stabbings when their home life is marginalised, their educational opportunities are disadvantaged and their peer group aspires to be no more than drug-dealers or gang members. As well as failing themselves, they are failed by society.

*　　*　　*

Another contemporary African-British dynasty that shares the African Victorian ancestry – which seems to have provided a blueprint for black empowerment – is the Casely-Hayford clan. Among them number: fashion designer Joe Casely-Hayford

OBE; curator and cultural historian Dr Augustus (Gus) Casely-Hayford; televison producer Peter; and his sister Margaret Casely-Hayford, director of legal services and company secretary for the John Lewis Partnership plc, who also sits on the board of NHS England.

The stellar siblings' father Victor Casely-Hayford trained as a barrister and went on to become an accountant. Their barrister uncle, Archie Casely-Hayford, served as Attorney-General of Ghana during the presidency of Kwame Nkrumah. The younger generation of Casely-Hayfords are following in their parents' footsteps, rather than resting on the familial laurels of their nineteenth-century antecedent Joseph Ephraim Casely Hayford MBE – a Ghanaian barrister who went on to become a notable pan-African statesman and his correspondingly illustrious wife. The 'African Victorian feminist' Adelaide Smith Casely-Hayford was born in Freetown, Sierra Leone in 1868. She was raised in England, received a secondary education in Jersey and attended a German university. After a quarter of a century spent abroad, Adelaide returned to Sierra Leone and established a school for girls. She was awarded an MBE for her public service contribution.

Education has always played a paramount role in the lives of a diverse group of African migrants to Britain – middle-class families from former British colonies such as Ghana, Kenya, Uganda and Nigeria. They may have arrived for economic or political reasons, but they were all drilled with the African mantra 'Education, Education, Education' (Tony Blair, please take note).

This helped combat a perception by certain white Britons that they should be treated as an underclass. In contrast to many households in Britain, black African homes were imbued with a work ethos and home environment conducive to intensive study and academic high achievement.

The non-profit organisation Excellence in Education (EIE) believes that 'an inner-city child is as good as any other' and offers two-hour extra-curricular lessons in subjects including maths, science and English across London on Saturday mornings. Significantly, several primary-aged African students at the EIE's centres of learning have broken national GCSE youngest pass records. Seven-year-old Marcus Ikpase, for example, who took part in a two-month EIE mentoring programme, was the youngest person to pass GCSE maths in 2013.

In the Independent Schools Council's 2013 Census category for 'new non-British pupils whose permanent homes are overseas', Nigerians and the rest of Africa ranked eighth (440 pupils) and eleventh (210 pupils) respectively. In the 'non-British pupils with parents living overseas' category, the Nigerian segment has grown in number by 16.3 per cent to 1,006 pupils since 2012. The rest of Africa share shrank by 1.2 per cent to 580 pupils, but, even so, their numbers were still higher than pupils from the US, central and South America, the Middle East and central Asia combined.

After the Chinese and Russians, Nigerians comprise the British private school sector's fastest-growing market segment, spending £300 million annually educating their children at

British schools and universities. If British children of Nigerian and other African extractions were included in these statistics, the number of private school pupils of black African extraction would be much higher. These figures are the tip of a global education iceberg and should come as no surprise; Nigerians are educational migrants who also fill US Ivy League universities en route to distinguished corporate, scientific and entrepreneurial careers. Billionaire business magnate Folorunsho Alakija, ranked by *Forbes* in 2013 as Nigeria's richest woman, with a net worth estimated at £1.5 billion, boarded as a child at the Welsh primary Dinorben School for Girls. She returned to Nigeria for a Muslim secondary education and then came back to Britain for secretarial college and fashion studies at the American College and the London School of Fashion. Her current £64 million London home at One Hyde Park is a far cry from the cold dorms of Llangernyw.

As Tinie Tempah's charismatic demeanour illustrated when high-fiving Prince William at the 2014 BAFTA ceremony, every Nigerian man is raised like a prince and usually has the confidence to shine academically and professionally whether schooled at Eton or the local comprehensive. Tempah, born Patrick Okogwu and raised on a Southwark council estate until the age of twelve, had this to say of his upbringing: 'I watched my parents go from having very basic jobs, to educating themselves, to buying a house. They set a really good bar for what they wanted their kids to achieve.'

Tempah attended a Catholic state school and worked hard

to attain the ten GCSEs and three A-levels that, although not prerequisite to a successful music career, have stood him in good stead to navigate the international music scene – and also ensured he had options to fall back upon if his entertainment career had stuttered. British-African trailblazers who took career routes divergent from the traditional bastions of medicine, law, engineering, accounting and science include: two British-Nigerians – artist Yinka Shonibare RA and telecoms tycoon Alexander Amosu (who are both of Yoruba extraction); British-Ghanaian fashion designer Ozwald Boateng; and British-Sudanese Roubi L'Roubi, owner of the Savile Row tailor Huntsman.

On the whole, African migrants prove industrious, whether opportunities lead them to the top of the corporate ladder – as in the case of Tidjane Thiam, the Ivorian chief executive of Prudential plc – or into more menial positions that also ensure they are the first and last people in the office block or the underground. Many 'invisible' African workers provide essential support services including catering, cleaning and maintenance, often for minimal wages.

Many undocumented African migrants – some of whom arrive for economic reasons, others fleeing persecution – have shared their shocking stories and dire circumstances via the blog Life Without Papers.

Illegal immigrant Ruth Asmah was trafficked into the UK as a fourteen-year-old by an aunt who used her as a domestic slave. She had believed her visit was a holiday; sadly, she was misinformed. Passed from household to household in the London area until she ran away at twenty, Ruth has managed to support herself and her young daughter by working without official documentation in Lancashire. She describes an impoverished life of living on as little as £125 per week, going hungry so that she can feed her daughter and 'constantly moving'. She adds, ' I don't take anything – no benefits, not even free school meals for Dyanna.' While working for Tesco on false papers, Ruth maintained a direct debit to Water Aid wishing to help those in worse situations in Africa. 'People think all kinds of things about immigrants – that we are like terrorists. But we don't mean any harm. We are just trying to do what's best for our families, for our kids. We are just people after all.'

Pursuers of peace and progress

With its former colonial ties and a shared knowledge and use of the English language, Britain has long offered a place of refuge for countless displaced Africans seeking asylum from civil and national wars. Recent embellishments to Britain's multicultural fabric include the South Sudanese, who were displaced by two civil wars that have claimed several million lives. In light of such conflicts, British asylum applications peaked in 1993 and then again in 2004. Most applications in the early 1990s were accepted; most after 1994 have been refused.

Southern Sudanese granted political asylum in Britain: Home Office statistics

YEAR	GRANTED	REFUSED
1989	45	5
1990	15	5
1991	15	10
1992	265	125
1993	1400	75
1994	50	145
1995	15	60
1996	65	95
1997	75	205
1998	55	65
1999	45	50
2000	155	395
2001	160	595
2002	175	455
2003	110	595
2004	155	1305
2005	90	900
2006	70	510
2007	80	305

The 2001 UK Census recorded 10,671 British residents who were born in South Sudan – making them the fifteenth-largest African migrant population in the UK. In 2006, the International Organization for Migration estimated the UK's South Sudanese population comprised between 10,000 and 25,000 residents in the capital, up to 18,000 in Brighton, 4,000 to 5,000 in the West Midlands, and 2,000 in Glasgow and Edinburgh.

Getty Images

Alek Wek.

Dinka refugee Alek Wek, one of the few globally successful and instantly recognisable African supermodels (although she is occasionally and inexplicably mistaken for British-Jamaican diva Naomi Campbell), recalls when her mother's limited cultural knowledge almost scuppered her stratospheric career. When Alek was scouted, her mother was shocked at the thought of her becoming a Page 3 girl; there were no fashion magazines back home, so she had no frame of reference. Like many refugees who make good, to Wek, education was the key to finding her place in a completely alien culture: 'I could never understand why other kids wanted to truant – my education here gave me everything. It's the place where I really got to flourish.'

A 2008 report by the internationally renowned Tavistock Centre entitled 'The Emotional Needs of Congolese Children in the Context of Educational Experiences' – commissioned by Camden Council's Children, Schools and Families Directorate – noted that, although 85 per cent of primary pupils and 82 per cent of Congolese secondary pupils were eligible for free school meals (compared to 42 per cent and 31 per cent of Camden pupils as a whole), their parents stressed that their standard of schooling in the Congo, prior to the outbreak of the civil wars, was very high. Indeed, it was 'much better than here'. This shows that parents had high aspirations for their children's futures, and worried about their school performance, despite their own struggles to find satisfactory employment. It is worth noting that 37.5 per cent of the parents questioned held a graduate degree gained in the Democratic Republic of Congo (DRC).

Citizens of the DRC – a former Belgian colony that still bears the scars of the havoc wreaked by King Leopold II's Congo Free State – were the largest refugee group in the UK in 1991. The Congolese arrived in Britain in three migratory waves, the first of which, in 1989, was composed of opponents to the authoritarian regime of President Mobutu.

The second wave came with the political instability surrounding the 1990–94 conflict in the DRC, which had led to considerable loss of life. This forced 74,000 Congolese, many from lower socio-economic classes than the first wave, to apply for asylum in Europe. Nearly a quarter of these applications were received by Britain, although it had no colonial link. Far from being a soft touch with asylum seekers – as many of my fellow citizens erroneously perceive – Britain recognised fewer Congolese asylum claims than other European states. Only 1 per cent of applicants were granted leave to remain on humanitarian grounds or refugee status.

The third and final wave of Congolese refugees came to flee the catastrophic effects of civil war in 1997. Those who received asylum tended to settle in London, particularly in Tottenham, where the melodic sounds of Lingala and the vibrant sights of sharp-dressed British-Congolese are now hallmarks of the area.

The rainbow migrants

Another problem of African immigration –
what should we do about Kelly Hoppen?

London is home to South Africa's largest western hemisphere expatriate community. Not only are they white, they tend to be affluent. Many of them live in London's prime residential districts, notably Highgate, Wimbledon and, latterly, Canary Wharf.

The 2001 UK Census recorded that 90 per cent of Britain's South African community were white; their ethnic origins were principally British or Afrikaner. South Africans of black and Indian origin comprised a modest 3 per cent while 'mixed' and 'other' amounted to 2 per cent.

Successful entrepreneur Stephen Schaffer grew up in apartheid-era South Africa. Seeing that his country was on 'tenterhooks with huge issues', he enrolled for post-graduate study at the London School of Economics in order to maintain his visa. After gaining his master's degree, Schaffer went on to co-found lingerie retail brand Knickerbox. Other white South African tycoons who have made their fortunes, or based themselves, in Britain include: internet pioneer Mark Shuttleworth; Gaydar founders Gary Frisch and Henry Badenhorst; interior designer Kelly Hoppen; and hotel magnate Sol Kerzner.

Perhaps one of the most famous South African names is Nicholas 'Nicky' F. Oppenheimer, the former De Beers and Diamond Trading Company chairman, who was born in South Africa in 1945 and then educated at Harrow School and Christ Church, Oxford. As well as dominating the global diamond trade, this scion of a famous dynasty focused his sparkling business acumen on acquiring a stake in mining company Anglo American plc, a conglomerate that has invested over £6 billion within the UK over the five-year period from 1 January 2008 to 31 December 2013 and has also paid £1.2 billion to the UK government in taxes within the same period. Anglo American happens to own half of Tarmac too, one of the UK's biggest construction materials businesses, and this subsidiary alone employs over 5,130 UK residents.

Nicky Oppenheimer is truly a master of London, as well as the universe: he is the only private individual currently permitted to commute by helicopter within the Square Mile of the City of London. Like many white South Africans in Britain,

Oppenheimer is of Jewish descent. In 2008, Runnymede, Britain's foremost race equality think tank, reported that an estimated 9 per cent of London's South African population are Jewish. The capital's Jewish population is reckoned to make up around 2 per cent of the total population.

Besides forging a successful business community, South Africans in Britain have contributed hugely to our culture and theatre. Many British national treasures are actually of South African origin. *Carry On* actor Sid James was born in the Hillbrow area of Johannesburg as Solomon Joel Cohen. Cherished television and radio presenter Bob Holness was born in Vryheid, a mining and ranching town in northern KwaZulu-Natal. Icons of British glamour, Jackie and Joan Collins, and Hollywood actress Sienna Miller share South African paternity as well as global acclaim. National newsreader Natasha Kaplinsky's father hails from South Africa by way of Poland.

In the world of politics, Peter Hain – the former Welsh Secretary and Secretary of State for Work and Pensions – was born in Kenya but raised in South Africa. Sir Laurens Jan van der Post CBE was born in the Orange River Colony and patriotically volunteered for the British Army. He became a Second World War hero and later advisor to British prime ministers. He received the honour of being chosen as one of Prince William's godfathers. Van der Post's love of Africa and his humanitarian and conservation legacies live on via his godson's campaigning and charitable activities, most notably the Prince William Award for Conservation in Africa.

Now, 21st-century Britain embraces the legend and legacy of departed black South African statesman Nelson Mandela, but this was not always the case.

During the apartheid era, black South Africans were reduced to non-citizens in their ancestral land by the 1970 Citizenship Act. Many exiles and fugitives sought refuge in Britain and strengthened the anti-apartheid movement, with fortification from Britain's existing black communities who were fighting their own battles against racism in British society.

The Somali surge

British Olympian Mo Farah.

Somalis seeking refuge from the regime of Siad Barre and the ensuing civil war in the 1980s were absorbed into an ethnic community established in Britain since 1869. Sailors from British Somaliland settled in port cities, particularly Cardiff, Liverpool and London, and worked in the expanding and prosperous dock neighbourhoods while they lived in Somali-run boarding houses. Another small wave of Somali seamen arrived with the Royal Navy during the Second World War; yet it is worth recording that, as late as 1953, there were only around 600 Somalis living in the UK.

This pioneer group of Somali migrants were mostly male; they were legally restricted to only work in the shipping industry – and even then, at rates that were 25 per cent below their British counterparts – and they were not permitted to settle in towns and cities that weren't shipping centres. The men viewed their time in Britain as temporary and so left their wives and families back home.

After the Second World War, when navy jobs diminished and there was a clamouring demand for labour to rebuild Britain, Somali men found work in industrial cities such as Manchester and Sheffield. As there was a boom in British industry and few Somali women to meet socially, the men sent for their wives and families. The community organisations established by Somali women in the 1960s and '70s were of great assistance to refugees fleeing here – the majority of Somali refugees arriving in Britain were women and children. Many of their husbands had been killed in the war or remained in Somalia to fight, while women joined husbands already resident in the UK. This influx of women changed the traditional composition of the migrant community and led to Britain hosting the world's largest Somali diaspora community, mostly residing in the East End of London. The UK has now become a 'meeting point' for exiled Somalis formerly based in other European nations as families reunify. The 2011 Census found that London, Birmingham and Bristol have the largest Somali-born populations with 65,333, 7,765 and 5,947 residents respectively.

One of the core strengths of the British-Somali community is their close-knit structure and supportive assistance to each other, which may have as much to do with a strong Islamic faith – predominantly Sunni – as it does with cultural factors. Somalis are one of the UK's largest Muslim groups and now operate several of their own mosques. Their united front is evident on many a British high street in the form of cafés offering internet services, halal meals, and tea and community sympathy. They are often staffed by multiple generations of the same family, utilising the old-school modus operandi of the many east African-Asian asylum seekers who laid the cornerstones of their current fortunes as shopkeepers. Will the Somalis follow their entrepreneurial lead? The Joseph Rowntree Foundation's 2007 report, 'Tackling Low Educational Achievement', found that Somalis underachieve at school in both primary and secondary learning. Could this record of low achievement – which, in turn, can lead to low self-esteem, isolation and a sense of alienation from the rest of society – be one of the key factors that motivate some young Somali males to join the criminal gangs and jihadist groups?

Somali culture has had a visible impact on British multiculturalism, legislation and politics. Hijab-wearing Somali females are about as prominent in London as businessmen in bowler hats once were. However, I personally doubt this latest in-your-face sartorial expression of identity will last long, with it being so severe a barrier to effective communication and empathy.

Nor will the cultural practice of female genital mutilation (FGM), which is also practised in some other African nations. This has become a feminist as well as a human rights issue in the UK. The London *Evening Standard* and *The Guardian* in particular have extensively covered the issue and campaigned to end the practice. Such campaigns are beginning to have an effect.

Edna Adan, a British-trained midwife and maternal health expert, served as both First Lady and Foreign Minister of Somaliland and first spoke out against FGM on Somali radio in the 1970s. Today, she is spearheading a new approach to ending FGM by targeting Somali men: 'It should not be a woman's affair. You can put your foot down if you are the head of the family.' Clearly the law in this area should be enforced with precious little sympathy for the expectations of imported culture. Although, in general, I am out to correct an imbalance in our perceptions of what comes with immigration, plainly not every cultural import is a good thing.

*   *   *

In the 1980s and '90s, Africans from Algeria, Angola, Ghana, Kenya, Nigeria and Sierra Leone sought asylum in Britain. The 2001 Census registered 17,048 Sierra Leonean-born residents in the UK. Yet, in fact, the Sierra Leonean presence in Britain is not so new. Many Sierra Leoneans, such as 92-year-old Noel Davies who served in the RAF during the Second World War, settled here in the past. Some notable mixed-race Britons are of Sierra Leonean extraction, from the composer Samuel Coleridge-Taylor – who was born in London in 1875 – to the Welsh Manchester United player Ryan Giggs OBE – who has a Sierra Leonean paternal grandfather. Sierra Leonean migrants are a diverse bunch of ethnic groups. University of London-educated, Sierra Leonean-Lebanese businessman Hisham Mackie's company H. M. Diamond accounted for 51 per cent of all official Sierra Leone diamond exports in 2004. After watching the feature movie *Blood Diamond*, many would assume that men born in Freetown who deal in diamonds would have hands just as dirty as the characters on the silver screen.

*   *   *

Border conflict between Ethiopia and Eritrea during the 1960s resulted in Ethiopia's expulsion of Eritreans. In 1976, the Eritrean Relief Association was formed in the UK (ERA UK) and provided services to Eritrean refugees alongside the United

Kingdom Immigration Advisory Services (UKIAS) and the Refugee Council (RC). Around 20,000 Eritrean asylum applications were made over twenty years and none were refused until 1993, when attitudes to refugees began to change. Sensational and politically charged terms – including 'welfare scroungers' and 'illegal immigrants' – began to be applied to asylum seekers.

Wealthy Ethiopians sought political asylum in Britain after the overthrow of Haile Selassie's government by a military junta in 1974. Ethiopians had long been free to study in the UK so many were familiar with British society. A second wave of Ethiopian migrants from a range of socio-economic backgrounds followed in 1991 after another civil war. In 2005, there were an estimated 20,000 full-descent Ethiopians in Britain, 84 per cent of them residing in London.

Unemployment levels are high. According to the BBC's 2008 Born Abroad immigration map, only 32.28 per cent of new Ethiopian immigrants were employed. Although 64.44 per cent of settled Ethiopians were in employment, the rate for British-born citizens of any ethnicity was 73.49 per cent.

Unemployment was not such a problem though for the polymath and actor Peter Ustinov. But of course he was British. Or was he Russian? Indeed, he once said, 'I have Russian, German, Spanish, Italian, French and Ethiopian blood in my veins.' His debated Ethiopian lineage is descended from Emperor Theodore II via the marriage of one of his daughters to a European engineer in imperial service to Ethiopia.

The Marquesses of Milford Haven also have some black blood mixed in with their aristocratic blue, since they count as ancestors of the Russo-Eritrean Major General Abram Petrovich Gannibal, great-grandfather of 'Russia's greatest poet' Alexander Pushkin. Pushkin was the great-grandfather of Nadejda Mikhailovna Mountbatten, Marchioness of Milford Haven and an aunt of Prince Philip, Duke of Edinburgh.

Nadejda Mikhailovna Mountbatten, Marchioness of Milford Haven.

A more noticeable sign of the times is that the Hon John Alexander Ladi Thynn, born in London in October 2014 to the Viscount and Viscountess of Weymouth, will one day become the 8th Marquess of Bath. Ladi, meaning 'more wealth', is a shortened form of the Yoruba forename Oladipo, in homage to his Nigerian grandfather – Oxford-educated businessman Oladipo Jadesimi.

One wonders if anyone is truly English, or even British. Is there anyone now who isn't mixed origin once you start tracing back? It is not a coincidence that the hugely popular BBC programme *Who Do You Think You Are?* so frequently struggles to stay within the country for long when exploring any particular lineage. After peeking beneath the surface of just a few, it is apparent that to attempt to partition the distinct geographical threads into neat homogeneous groups would be a gross simplification. In fact, let me put it more simply: it's total nonsense.

Chapter 5

The south Asian community

IN 21ST-CENTURY BRITAIN, THE CHARACTERISTICS
and contributions of immigrants from the Indian subcontinent have become hallmarks of what is considered modern
British culture and success. In 2014, the most common surname for a British doctor registered with the General Medical
Council was Khan – which fittingly translates as 'leader' in
the Asian language of Pashto. In second place was the Guja-
rati surname Patel. Ahmed and Ali were also ranked within
the top ten list.

Moreover, many of the personalities whose success stories are covered in the media have south Asian names – and even titles. A considerable cluster now sits in the House of Lords. For example: Lord Paul, the business tycoon who sits on the Labour benches; Lord Karan Bilimoria of Chelsea, the beer baron; and Baroness Sayeeda Warsi, the leading Conservative politician who is of Pakistani ethnicity.

The south Asian community has made a considerable impact on business as well as politics. They are now among the wealthiest and most successful people in Britain. The Hinduja brothers – Sri and Gopi – now rank as the wealthiest billionaires based in Britain according to the 2014 *Sunday Times* Rich List. Other prominent Asian success stories include the Mittal family, who have created one of the world's biggest steel companies, and Perween Warsi CBE, the founder of S&A Foods, which supplies to major supermarkets. Both of these families boast Indian origin.

Meanwhile, telecommunications tycoon Gulu Lalvani – whose Binatone company introduced the first cordless telephones to Europe in 1996 – is of Pakistani origin. Restaurateur Atique Choudhury, whose venture Yum Yum has become Europe's largest Thai restaurant, Moorad Choudhry – a senior managing director at the Royal Bank of Scotland plc – and Aref Karim – a hedge fund manager – are all British-Bengalis who have made their mark on UK business and the wider global economy too.

Immigrants from the Indian subcontinent: how education has driven success

No less than 43 per cent of Indians work in professions such as law and accountancy, while 11 per cent of Indian women in the UK hold higher managerial positions. Could this be the reason why nearly a quarter (24 per cent) of Indians were found most likely to vote Conservative, compared with 6 per cent of black Africans?

The success of so many Indian migrants should serve as proof to more marginalised segments of their wider community that breaking through glass ceilings is indeed possible with unshakeable self-belief, higher educational qualifications and tenacious career-building.

However, looked at overall, the immigrant community from what was previously West and East Pakistan have fared less well. The statistics reveal that almost a quarter (24 per cent) of Pakistani men are employed as minicab and taxi drivers, while 35 per cent of Bangladeshis have low-skill occupations – and nearly half of them work in the restaurant sector, whether offering tandoori dishes or other fare. Their wives tend not to work; indeed, 42 per cent of Bangladeshi women have never worked, neither have 39 per cent of Pakistani women. They tend to manage hearth and home and many may be confronted by language and patriarchal barriers if they venture out and search for work opportunities.

Bangladeshi and Pakistani migrants have tended to lag behind immigrants from India because of a combination of factors, notably more disadvantaged backgrounds, a higher incidence of poverty and the fact that English is very much a second language. Yet there has been a noticeable improvement in educational attainment in recent years. This includes a 22 per cent leap forward in attainment of five GCSE A*–C grades (including maths and English) from 2006/07 to 2012/13.

* * *

Perhaps Bangladeshi and Pakistani students will match Indians as educational outperformers in the longer term. After all, the number of affluent Pakistani, Sri Lankan and Bangladeshi pupils attending UK independent schools is beginning to match the figure for the better-established and well-heeled Indian community, who have long sent their children to elite British schools.

Destination of pupils after Key Stage 5 (A-levels)

	SOME FORM OF EDUCATION (%)	HIGHER EDUCATION (%)
White	62	43
Indian	81	70
Pakistani	77	62
Bangladeshi	76	63
Black African	79	66
Black Caribbean	71	53

Source: Policy Exchange.

South Asian entrepreneurial flair – in conjunction with an inherent dedication to education – is a subcontinental trait that has undoubtedly made a major contribution to Britain's economic clout. Indeed, they represent a blueprint, which newer migrant groups would do well to follow for longer-term success. More to the point, indigenous white Britons themselves would be well advised to shape up and follow the modus operandi of south Asian migrants (and other migrant groups). The educational league tables reveal that working-class white people are falling significantly behind immigrant groups. David Aaronovitch, writing in *The Times*, observed that 'the model of migrant miscreance is now not the smelly, feckless, uneducated, crime-prone chancer, but the hard-working, job- and school-lace-snatching overachiever. The problem with migrants is not their inability, but their ability relative to some of the indigenous population.'

It is telling to discover that every single minority group in Britain has a higher proportion of students remaining in formal education at the ages of sixteen and eighteen than the white population. The statistics speak for themselves. According to the Department for Education's National Pupil Database for the year 2013, 70 per cent of Indians, 63 per cent of Bangladeshis and 62 per cent of Pakistani students went on to higher education after receiving A-level qualifications – a stark contrast to the much lower figure of 43 per cent of white students who went on to college or university. Furthermore, 37 per cent of Indian students attended the top tier of British universities – a far higher proportion than those from the black Caribbean community.

The south Asian community: what the latest Census and market research data tells us

The 2011 UK Census recorded that Asian and Asian-British citizens account for 7.5 per cent of the total population. It is important to note that those with Chinese ancestry (about 400,000 of them) were no longer categorised as 'other' and became incorporated into the Asian-British category. After white British and 'any other white', Indian was the third-largest British ethnic group, totalling 1.4 million people (2.5 per cent). Pakistani came second, with 2 per cent of the overall total (1.1 million), while the Bangladeshi community grew by a remarkable 56 per cent to around 450,000 in the decade between the 2001 and 2011 Census.

The south Asian population have packed a cultural punch far greater than their numbers. They number almost 3 million, yet 23 million Britons regularly eat curry. Could a litmus test for migrant assimilation be via the stomach? Pilau rice is recognised and relished by most Britons, but they would probably have more trouble identifying the piquant jolloff rice favoured by the west African community. The colonial writers who contributed to *The Complete Indian Housekeeper and Cook*, published in 1888, could hardly have foreseen the cuisine of Kolkata and Lahore being devoured with delight by Englishmen from Land's End to John o'Groats in the twenty-first century.

Nowadays, curry has been adopted as one of Britain's national dishes. Asian food is now a big part of the nation's staple diet, as families opt for international cuisine over British dishes three out of seven nights a week. According to a market research survey undertaken for Food Network UK, nine in ten of the UK's favourite international meals are Asian. Indeed, surveys regularly show that chicken tikka masala is one of the country's favourite meal choices. Over 9,000 restaurants nationwide meet the country's appetite for what were once exotic and hard-to-find spices. National Curry Week, devoted to the dishes from Britain's most culinary-favoured migrant group, attests to the special place migrants from the Indian subcontinent have carved for themselves in British society, their impact upon a once unadventurous palette, and the evolution and acceptance of multiculturalism.

The presence of south Asian migrants has changed more than just national tastes, though. The retail culture that we take for granted – 24-hour and Sunday service with a fast turnaround of purchasable goods – was forged by the hard-working Asian political migrants – often Indian Gujaratis, cast out of Uganda by that murderous mountebank Idi Amin. Their dedication and service has increased the efficiency, effectiveness and tax revenues of this 'nation of shopkeepers' and ensured that drinking tea with no milk on a Sunday is a distant memory.

Religion: is Britain still a Christian country?

According to the Archbishop of Canterbury Justin Welby, Britain remains a 'deeply Christian country', although his predecessor Rowan Williams described us as a 'post-Christian' nation. What is certainly the case is that head teachers in cities with large Muslim populations – notably Bradford, Manchester and the East End of London – have raised deeply felt concerns regarding attempts to infiltrate state schools with radical Islamic beliefs and practices, including the illegal segregation of male and female pupils as sanctioned by Sharia law.

Then Education Secretary Michael Gove ordered an inquiry into Birmingham schools after an inspection of one of them – Park View secondary school – found that girls were segregated at the back of the classroom. The same school had invited an extremist preacher to lecture the pupils, and GCSE syllabuses were 'restricted to comply with a conservative Islamic teaching' approach to subject matters.

The current Archbishop of Canterbury is well aware that, in modern Britain, relatively few Christians attend church but an Anglican education remains popular. It is striking to note that nearly a million pupils attend Church of England schools and that, within this large, diverse group, a significant proportion are Muslim immigrants. Indeed, some C of E schools have an intake of over 80 per cent from the Muslim community, the majority of whom tend to be from a south Asian background.

The Church of England states that it is committed to 'Faith in the System' and promotes community cohesion through schooling. This commitment is illustrated in the reservation of 25 per cent of places in new C of E schools 'for pupils from the local neighbourhood regardless of faith background or none'.

Ironically, despite the welcoming of Muslims into the

classroom, their religious norms are not as welcome in the Church of England's school canteens. In 2011, the General Synod advised Church of England schools to ensure that only non-halal meat is served due to halal consumption 'spreading the practice of Sharia law' throughout Britain. Such a stance is in stark contrast to an emerging trend spotted by the *Daily Mail*, who, in May 2014, railed against 'A stealthy takeover of Britain's supermarket shelves: Unlabelled halal meat has become the "default" position.' In response to the public outcry, the Conservative government tabled an amendment to the Consumer Rights Bill that would require a move to clearer food labelling.

Hindu Diwali celebrants.

It is generally assumed that the strong religious cultures within south Asian communities are a key factor and constant touchstone in the economic success and community cohesion they enjoy. For their part, Indians have the most religious diversity, with a spread of 45 per cent Hindu, 22 per cent Sikh and 14 per cent Muslim, compared to Bangladeshi and Pakistani communities who are almost wholly Muslim. Indians are two to three times more likely than other BME groups to state that religion makes little or no difference to their lives. Incidentally, this ratio is the same as the religiously inclined black African community. Religious values may simply be an unconscious part of life – as unnoticeable as breathing – like it was in earlier eras of religious devotion. Market research records that 70 per cent of south Asians claim religion plays a major part in their lives, whereas only 14 per cent of white Britons would admit to the same feeling of faith.

What history tells us: the Roma community

South Asians' influence on Britain goes far deeper than the recent erection of mosques and the long-term establishment of retail emporia. Many historic south Asian stories are categorised within the experiences of other migrant groups: the first migrants of south Asian origin to enter Britain were the travelling Roma people, more commonly known as gypsies. Their origins in the marginalised Dalit caste of India was confirmed by scientists from Hyderabad's Centre for Cellular and Molecular Biology, who collaborated with geneticists in Estonia and

Switzerland to compare over 10,000 samples from 214 different Indian ethnic groups with Roma men in Europe.

'We are Britain's first non-resident Indian community,' said Britain's Gypsy Council spokesman Joseph Jones, when his group's origins were confirmed. He added, 'We're not outcasts here. I don't care if we are associated with Dalits – I don't live in a community where caste exists. I do feel a bit Indian, I've always felt an affinity with Indians.'

As with many migrant trajectories, the Roma have travelled and settled around the world – and continue to do so – to escape persecution and achieve a higher standard of living. Their westbound exodus that continues within the EU zone – much to the chagrin of Park Lane residents and metropolitan law enforcement – began in the eleventh century, when they fought as soldiers in wars in what is now Punjab. They later fled the fall of Hindu kingdoms in what is now Pakistan, and may also have sought refuge from the rise of Islam within the Indian subcontinent.

First noticed in Britain in the sixteenth century – and noted for their craftsmanship, horse-dealing and trading skills – will the Roma, who share a root origin with Britain's more recent south Asian migrants, be recognised and accepted by their new-found kin who have little in common with them culturally?

*　*　*

It is true to say that south Asian history in Britain may well be obscured. There have been more Africans than Asians in Britain since 1500, so many south Asian and Chinese people were referred to as 'black' in official records. To be referred to as 'inde' in early modern English records usually denoted Native American ancestry. The south Asian/Indian presence became noticeable in its own right when Indians migrated to these shores during Britain's initial trade with, and later colonisation of, India.

Britain's involvement in India began in the 1700s and occurred in two phases. Coastal trading with Indians took place in the first half of the century but soon gave way to military campaigns of remorseless attrition across eastern and southeastern India after the 1750s. The wealthy province of Bengal was the first of many to be conquered by the British. Later campaigns seized territories extending from the Ganges Valley up to Delhi, as well as across the southern India peninsula. Further British military domination ended in the subjugation of the remaining Indian states in fewer than fifty years. By the turn of the century, Britain dominated the whole of the subcontinent, with indigenous rulers bowing to the might of the East India Company, which was originally founded under a royal charter granted by Queen Elizabeth in 1600. The company exploited its monopoly of all English trade to Asia and was soon sending up to thirty ships a year, generating annual sales revenue of £2,000,000 – an astronomical fortune at the time.

Indian cotton became the core of the East India Company's trade in the late eighteenth century, with cloth woven by Indian weavers imported into Britain in vast quantities to meet the global demand for cheap, lightweight and washable fabric for clothing and upholstery. India's artisanship and sophisticated economy allowed opportunities for enterprising Englishmen to make their fortunes exporting agricultural products, including indigo, sugar and opium. These pioneering entrepreneurs collaborated with wealthy Indian merchants and bankers to make considerable fortunes.

Britons who had made their fortune in India returned home accompanied by their south Asian servants, who continued to serve them as domestics, nannies and *ayah* nursemaids. The captains and officers of the East India Company's vessels developed a taste for Indo-Portuguese dishes. Consequently, they brought local cooks back home to England to satisfy their appetites. They did not all cope with Britain's climate and way of life, though: thirteen Indo-Portuguese cooks died and were buried within the parish of St Nicholas at Deptford in the year 1797 alone.

The first British citizens of Indian descent turn out to be the Goans of Bombay. When the Portugese Princess Catherine of Braganza married King Charles II in 1662, the 'Merry Monarch' promptly loaned Bombay – now Mumbai – to the East India Company. As subjects of the Portuguese empire, many Goans were Christian. East Greenwich baptism records suggest that a minority of young Indians from the Malabar Coast were employed as house servants in late seventeenth-century London.

Aristocrats such as Lady Charlotte Fitzroy – Charles II's illegitimate daughter by his mistress – and Barbara Villiers – Duchess of Cleveland – recruited Indian pages as well as African 'blackamoors'. It can be argued that non-white skin and servitude were employed as visual and social foils to enhance the whiteness and wealth of noble ladies throughout Europe.

Two centuries later, English mistress and Indian servant race relations had gone from strength to strength. Queen Victoria was particularly attached to her Sikh Indian manservant, Abdul Karim. 'I am so very fond of him. He is so good and gentle and understanding … and is a real comfort to me,' the Queen wrote in 1888 to her daughter-in-law, the Duchess of Connaught. At the time, Karim was twenty-six; the Empress of India was seventy.

Queen Victoria, who never visited her subjects on the sub-continent, nonetheless delighted in her evening Urdu lessons with her closest companion Karim – and the rest of the royal household made do with the spice of curry added to their extensive and multi-coursed dinner menus.

Luckily for Abdul Karim, Queen Victoria permitted him to bring his wife to England and gave the couple a cottage on each of her estates, even building 'Karim Cottage' in his honour in the grounds of Balmoral.

The thousands of lascars, originally Indo-Portuguese in origin – who arrived in Britain courtesy of the East India Company over a period of two centuries – were not so lucky. Mainly Bengalis and/or Muslims (like Karim), they took white British brides due to the absence of Indian women. They were able to indulge their appetite for exotic spices when a Bengali, Sake Dean Mahomed, opened London's first Indian restaurant – the Hindoostane Coffee House. This might be viewed as the forerunner of Britain's balti boom centuries later.

Not one to base his success on a sole good or service, Sake Dean Mahomed diversified his business portfolio and is said to be responsible for introducing therapeutic massage and shampoo to Britain.

By the mid-1800s, over 40,000 Indians are estimated to have been residing in Britain. Seamen, businessmen, diplomats, soldiers, students, scholars and tourists made up a population that was estimated to have risen to as many as 70,000 in 1900. During the First World War it is reckoned that 51,616 lascar seamen were living in Britain.

The Indian Army made a huge contribution to the First World War: a million troops were present in several divisions and independent brigades across Europe, the Mediterranean and Middle East. A total of 74,187 Indian soldiers lost their lives fighting the German and Ottoman empires, on behalf of Britain, on the Western Front and in east Africa. Until 1911, Indian soldiers were ineligible for the Victoria Cross and were decorated with the Indian Order of Merit, a legacy from the days of the East India Company. However, Khudadad Khan, who served with the 129th Duke of Connaught's Own Baluchis, was the first Indian recipient awarded the Victoria Cross in any conflict.

As was the case with African and Afro-Caribbean seamen and servicemen after the First World War, Commonwealth patriots from the Indian subcontinent also sadly faced discrimination after demobilisation. British workers were particularly disgruntled with the excess number of 'coloured' seamen – the number of lascars was especially noticeable – as well as the lack of jobs. South Asians were a particular target for racial hatred due to the high levels of competition for work. Indians, who were paid much lower rates than their white British counterparts, were charged with 'stealing' English jobs, and this hostility triggered debates in Parliament. Interracial relationships and marriage with local white women further provoked indigenous hostility. The race riots of 1919 saw south Asians attacked, but not as much as black and Chinese residents who were seen as more of a threat. In May 1919, the doors at West India Dock Road's Strangers' Home for Asiatics, Africans, and South Sea Islanders had to be barred. South Asian men were escorted through the hostile mob by uniformed police and south Asian businesses were also targeted for attack.

Indian troops in Burma in 1944.

When Britain declared war on Nazi Germany in September 1939, British India – comprising Bangladesh, India and Pakistan – sent two million volunteer soldiers to fight the Axis powers under British command. Several Indian princely states, including Bikaner, Hyderabad, Jaipur and Kashmir, provided sizeable donations to the war effort. Princely states also provided a quarter of a million troops for active service with the Indian State Forces (ISF). These units served Britain in Burma, Italy, Malaya, the Middle East and north Africa, as well as providing garrison and security within India. Five ISF battalions were within the garrison of Singapore upon its fall to the Japanese in February 1942.

Yet it is important to stress that not all Indians were strong supporters of the colonial power. A sizeable minority fought for the Axis powers and the Japanese. Indeed, around three-quarters of the 40,000 Indian troops captured in Singapore in February 1942 subsequently joined the pro-independence Indian National Army, the military wing of Rash Behari Bose's Indian National League. These troops fought against Allied forces in the Burma Campaign, as well as in the northeast Indian regions of Kohima and Imphal. Furthermore, some of the Indian troops captured when Singapore fell became PoW camp guards at Changi jail. Bose's namesake – Subhas Chandra Bose – was the leader of the radical wing of the Indian National Congress in the late 1920s and '30s. Throughout the war years he actively co-operated with the Axis powers who, in return, gave his movement both financial and military support in its long-running campaign for Indian independence.

The post-war character of immigration: an entirely new dynamic

South Asian migration prior to the Second World War had been small, mainly temporary, yet at times magnificently affluent. As members of the empire, visas were not required, so, for the regal Indian elite, Britain was a choice destination for leisure and serious spending. The Indian maharajas poured vast sums into the coffers of British luxury goods companies, including Asprey, Bentley and Wedgwood. This consumption had a noticeable trickle-down effect after the First World War. Motoring expert Murad Ali Baig says that, of the 20,000 Rolls-Royces produced before the Second World War, 20 per cent of them were exported to British-ruled India.

The Indian Maharaja of Patiala commissioned Asprey to produce enormous teak travelling trunks lined with blue velvet – and filled with silver bathing utensils with ornate tiger-head waterspouts – for each of his wives in the 1920s. This one order kept a clutch of specialist craftsman busy as the Depression loomed.

As well as commissioning extravagant objects for everyday use, south Asian royals patronised the leading British artists of the day and influenced style internationally. For example, fashion icon Maharani Sita Kumari of Kapurthala – a muse of Cecil Beaton, the celebrated English society photographer – influenced Elsa Schiaparelli, and was one of the best customers in Parisian couture houses.

Maharani Gayatri Devi of Jaipur, whose English governesses had been recommended by Queen Mary, received part of her education in England and Switzerland. She grew up to be named one of the 'Ten Most Beautiful Women in the World' by *Vogue* magazine, and was a much-respected philanthropist.

Belonging to royal stock and spending vast sums of money did not stop racism from rearing its ugly head, but personal wealth enabled India's aristocracy to wreak their revenge if they encountered discrimination. For instance, when the Nizam of Hyderabad was insulted by a showroom salesman at a Rolls-Royce dealership (when he enquired about a car while casually dressed), he returned – in his royal costume – to purchase all the models available in the showroom. They were promptly shipped off to India and used as refuse trucks within his municipality. The resulting bad press damaged Rolls-Royce's reputation worldwide. The owners of the silver lady marque apologised for the racist treatment and asked him to decommission the luxury rubbish trucks. By way of inducement, he was offered six free replacements. The lesson to be drawn is that hitting companies in the pocket gives a black eye to discrimination. Decades later, marginalised south Asian migrants working in car factories across Britain would prove this point when they opted to take industrial action.

The post-war picture

After the Second World War ended in 1945, Mr Attlee's Labour government concluded that a large-scale influx of immigrant labour would be required to reconstruct the beleaguered British economy. In 1949, the Royal Commission on Population stated that Britain would welcome 'without reserve' migrants of 'good stock'. British subjects from Commonwealth regions including south Asia, Africa and the Caribbean answered this invitation and supplied the UK with the labour it craved.

It was in this post-war era of the 1950s and '60s that Britain experienced its first large-scale immigration from outside Europe. Many south Asian migrants arrived from the newly formed states of India and Pakistan, which were created by 'partition' when Britain withdrew from the subcontinent in 1947. Immigrants from the Indian subcontinent – who were seen as one group by many white Britons – were, in reality, a diverse group in terms of social class, culture and religious background. Hindus mainly migrated from western India's Gujarat region; Sikhs from their eastern heartland in the Punjab; and the majority of Muslims from West Pakistan, with some coming from what was then known as East Pakistan (later to be renamed Bangladesh in 1972).

The demand for labour from the Commonwealth, combined with uncertain economic prospects at home, led to a surge in immigration in the 1950s from the Indian subcontinent. Many of the doctors recruited by the NHS in the early 1960s, when Enoch Powell was the Conservative Health Minister, were Hindus from

India. He needed their skilled help to sustain the NHS, which was already showing signs of significant stress. I would suggest that the skilled hands of Indian doctors prevented rivers of blood being shed by English patients.

Sikh migrants from India's Punjab region had a strong British connection. As soldiers in army units, they had seen active service in both world wars within elite regiments, and many had been sent to other colonies within the British empire. Men who had previously been employed in the police force and colonial army welcomed the opportunity to migrate to Britain as they were mainly from peasant families. In England, they found jobs in the manufacturing and textile industries, and some even obtained work in the service sectors – a majority at west London's Heathrow airport. After the Commonwealth Immigrant Act of 1962 restricted their freedom of movement, most south Asian workers settled in Britain and sent for their families to join them when they were able to do so.

Pakistani migrant Mahmood Sultan entered Britain in a state of anxiety: 'I couldn't really believe I was really going to England,' he recounts, 'because to go to England used to be the prerogative of rulers, of the Indian subcontinent rajas and maharajas and Nawabs, an ordinary person like me, we could only visit England in our dreams.'[5]

The majority of Britain's Pakistani migrants originated from

---

5 Source: http://www.connectinghistories.org.uk/Learning%20Packages/Migration/migra-tion_settlement_20c_lp_02.asp

Mirpur in Kashmir. The city had a long tradition of providing manpower for British ships and some of them had settled in Britain in the earlier part of the twentieth century. Post-war immigration was different: many Pakistani migrants found employment in the textile industries in the north of England. Bradford and Lancashire mill towns, such as Blackburn and Bolton, along with other towns in Greater Manchester and Yorkshire, remain strongholds of the British Pakistani community. The West Midlands and Birmingham communities were established by men working in the car manufacture and engineering industries; the Luton and Slough communities by men employed in light industrial trade.

The British Pakistani community grew four-fold during the 1960s: a total population of 31,000 in 1961 climbing to 136,000 in 1971. Many were attracted by the jobs available in England; some sought refuge from Pakistan's war with India in 1965; others chose to make Britain their new home when parts of the Mirpur district were submerged after the Mangla dam was built in 1966. A significant proportion of these Pakistani migrants came to take up posts and train within the NHS. This underlines the fact that the NHS has been heavily reliant throughout its history on employees from the Commonwealth – many of them well-qualified doctors, nurses and technicians. Without them, Britain's favourite legacy of the Attlee era would be on life support.

It is worth emphasising that Britain experienced large inflows of south Asian migrants as a result of African members of the

Commonwealth expelling their immigrant populations. Pan-African sentiments running through post-imperial African states tended to adopt a form of pan-Africanism that threatened the Asian communities who had prospered in countries such as Kenya and Uganda. When President Jomo Kenyatta launched a programme of Africanisation in Kenya, 23,000 citizens of Asian descent left the country in the period between 1965 and 1967. These refugees triggered a great deal of hostility from the indigenous community when they arrived in the UK with their British passports. Consequently, the 1968 Commonwealth Immigrants Act was hurried through Parliament in order to counter the mass arrival of east African refugees – not one of the nation's finest moments.

Ugandan-Asians arrive at Stansted airport in 1972.

The passing of a further Immigration Act in 1971 included the contentious legal 'patriality' concept. This legal edict restricted entry for south Asian migrants unless they had a parent or grandparent born, adapted or naturalised in the UK. Hence, the unconditional citizenship African-Asians had enjoyed when African states gained their independence in 1963 was now well and truly null and void. The barriers had gone up.

When Uganda's leader Idi Amin forcibly expelled the country's minority Indian and Pakistani community on 4 August 1972 (via an order to leave the country within ninety days), over half of the Asian community of that country held British passports with the accompanying right to enter and reside in Britain. Despite Edward Heath's Conservative government's initial reluctance to see the resettlement of Ugandan-Asians, Britain did accept 28,000 of the 80,000 citizens whom President Amin had ejected from his country. The UK government engineered their resettlement in order to 'relieve the burden' and deflate the pressure upon social services in certain localities. Ugandan-Asians were steered away from the existing Asian community hubs of London and Leicester, with which they were socially networked. The host country was divided between 'red' and 'green' locations, but only 38 per cent accepted accommodation in the 'green' areas in which they were encouraged to settle.

Most Ugandan-Asians had lived in relative prosperity within a cosseted and close-knit community in a technicolour tropical paradise. Yasmin Alibhai-Brown evocatively describes it in her memoir of migration and food *The Settler's Cook Book.* Leaving at such short notice had put the majority at a great financial disadvantage. Fearing the freezing of their assets beforehand, savings had been put into gold jewellery to be liquidated in the future. However, this capital – as well as their properties, valuable possessions and stock-in-trade – was often left behind when the migrants fled for their lives.

Drab, cold and hostile Britain was a shock to both culture and the system. Alibhai-Brown recounts stepping off the plane to a welcome from 'lines of "patriots" with obscene placards'. She says, 'Contrary to popular myth, we were never "refugees" received with British generosity, but people conned by the state into opting for passports that were rendered worthless.'

The number of Ugandan-born Asians entering Britain rose by 270 per cent between 1971 (12,000) and 1981 (45,000); the Ugandan crisis also spilled over to affect south Asians in other east African nations. The 2011 UK Census registered that 44 per cent of Ugandan-born residents arrived during the 1970s. A figure of 31 per cent of Britain's 35,000-strong Tanzanian population in 2011 also reported having arrived between 1971 and 1980.

The influx of African-Asians was met with goodwill by some, and hostility by others. Their entry came at a time of economic difficulty marked by high unemployment. Harsh public criticism of non-white immigration became the norm. An estimated total of 1,400 Londoners came out to demonstrate against the 'invasion of Britain' and the cost to the nation.

However, Mr Heath's government and some national news-papers swayed support towards the refugees by painting Idi Amin as the 'black Hitler' and emphasising the economic benefits to be gained by welcoming the middle-class migrants into British society. Today, some Ugandan-Asian households whose prosperity is based on their opportunity and success in revitalising the shopkeeping trade adorn portraits of Edward Heath with garlands of faux marigolds.

Conservative MP Shailesh Vara praised the dignity, deter-mination and hard work of his father and other Ugandan migrants of the era during the fortieth anniversary of the exodus in 2012:

> Rather than looking at their expulsion as life-destroying, they saw it as a setback. They didn't stay downcast – got up and started over again. I remember Ugandan-Asian men laughing because English businesses closed at 5 p.m., had weekends off, even. They opened shops that never shut and transformed consumer expectations across Britain.

Mr Vara suggested to Yasmin Alibhai-Brown in a *Financial Times* interview that the racism he experienced as a boy grow-ing up in Birmingham had been the spur to his success. Upon spotting a 'No Wogs' sign in a house window, he committed himself to succeeding in life. Another interviewee who was attacked by racist thugs and received no help from the police now employs one of his assailants as his gardener.

As non-white people, post-Second World War communities of south Asian origin used the term 'black' in alliance with their African and Caribbean migrant counterparts in their struggle against institutional racism and racist skinhead movements. The combined efforts of the black and Asian communities to combat racism during the difficult decades – the 1960s, '70s and '80s – reaped major dividends for minority ethnic groups in the areas of education, employment and politics. The factory strikes of the 1960s and '70s appear to have improved the lot of many low-paid black and Asian workers.

The Asian communities actively supported strikers: temples offered free food; landlords waived rents; and grocers allowed relaxed credit in a move to strengthen strikers' bid to negotiate equality. These campaigning efforts were accompanied by a robust body of race relations legislation, including a succession of Race Relations Acts (1965, 1968, 1976 and 2000) to counteract racial discrimination in the workplace and elsewhere. The Commission for Racial Equality, created as part of the 1976 Race Relations Act, endeavoured to put equality principles into practice.

The formation of the Black Sections of the Labour Party in 1983 was a lesson in the strength created via unity: African, Asian and Caribbean men and women carried on the legacy of Shapurji Saklatvala, the first black Labour MP who was elected to Parliament in 1922 from Battersea North. At present, the majority of minority ethnic Members of Parliament and the House of Lords are of south Asian ethnicities.

*   *   *

Britain also experienced two further major waves of south Asian migration. The mass 'asylum seeking' – that has become a political hot potato for both the Labour and Conservative governments – began with an influx of Tamil refugees in 1985. The second wave was linked to emigration from Bangladesh.

Small numbers of professional migrants from Sri Lanka (Ceylon until 1972) had entered Britain during the 1960s and '70s. They were well-educated, affluent, model migrants who had found success and established themselves within the health service and in white-collar professions. The anti-Tamil riots of 1983 exacerbated the tensions between Sri Lanka's majority Sinhalese and minority Tamil communities, and escalated into a civil war between the Sri Lankan government and the Liberation Tigers of Tamil Eelam. Many poor Sri Lankans sought refuge in nearby India, but those with better means and family connections sought sanctuary from state persecution in the UK.

Britain had not received such a large number of asylum applications from the New Commonwealth since the Ugandan crisis. As before, the Conservative government implemented further restrictive legislation and immigration policies. Visas were soon required by visitors from Sri Lanka. In 1987, after a high-profile deportation case of fifty-eight Tamils who had sought asylum via fraudulent representations, the Carriers' Liability Act was passed imposing £1,000 fines on any airlines or shipping companies ensuring passage without correct documentation. The fine was doubled in 1992.

Despite these moves to erect even higher barricades, the Tamil community has grown in strength, with its highest concentration found in the capital – most notably Newham, an east London borough that is home to a vibrant Tamil micro-economy full of enterprising small- and medium-sized businesses. Indeed, London accounts for 70 per cent of the UK Tamil population.

The Tamil community's voice, political cause and evolution in British culture is heard worldwide in the urban lyrics and London-tinged sound of controversial female rapper M.I.A. She has used her global profile to bring attention to the Tamil cause and the politics of Sri Lanka. Another Tamil immigrant, Melani Dimple, was, until recently, the Queen's personal housemaid at Buckingham Palace.

Getty Images

M.I.A. is a voice of modern Britain who has cracked the US. She was born Mathangi Arulpragasam in Hounslow, west London.

The final south Asian group to migrate to Britain on a large scale is the Bangladeshi community. The partitioning of India after independence from Britain created the new state of Pakistan. The two territories that comprised Pakistan – West Pakistan (which remains Pakistan today) and East Pakistan (now Bangladesh) – had a fractious relationship that resulted in a civil war beginning in 1970 (and ending in 1971 with the creation of Bangladesh).

During the civil war, the majority of Bangladeshi families currently in the UK sought refuge in Britain from the Sylhet region. Many were housed alongside white working-class 'cockney' Londoners in council estates across the East End – an area still bearing the architectural scars of the Second World War Blitz. As we have seen, the area had long been the starting point for many migrants fleeing persecution – from French Huguenots to Jews fleeing Nazi Europe.

Bangladeshi men at first found it easy to gain employment within the steel and textile mills around the UK. When these industries collapsed, the men fell back on the skills they had honed back home, including tailoring and jewellery trading. One skill from home had a revolutionary effect on their fortunes and national tastes – catering. The appreciation and marketing of 'Indian' food, and the ensuing boom in 'Indian' restaurants and takeaways, should really be re-titled 'Bangladeshi'.

An unsavoury note to the nation's favourite dishes was uncovered behind the scenes of several Brick Lane curry houses in 2014. Banglatown is home to many successful Bangladeshi businesses, but also imprisons some of the most marginalised migrants in

Britain. A Bengali businessman interviewed by the *Daily Mail* described the plight of the 'invisible' catering staff of Bangla-town – the affectionate name given to the locale of curry houses around east London's Brick Lane – as 'modern-day slavery'.

To sate the appetite of Britain's curry lovers, and send back the billions of pounds remitted to Sylhet from overseas each year, hundreds of thousands of Bengali men have migrated. The kitchens of the UK's Indian restaurants are the end destinations for most.

Brick Lane.

Some men are graduates, unable to find jobs at home. Many pay enormous sums to arrange their migration, which may take decades for their families to pay back. This investment is made for the long-term prosperity of the family. Why else become indebted for £10,000 if your weekly income is less than

£5? Families are tricked to believe that their sons will easily be able to afford to pay back £350 per week when in Britain. They might if they were paid the minimum wage and received their earnings – but many do not. As soon as the UK restaurateur receives the British work permit – usually for one year – the new employee is ensnared. Some men are viewed lucky to receive even £30 for working a sixty-hour week. It has been suggested that as many as 10,000 men may be in this treacherous position in London alone.

'The longest time I had work was five weeks, at a restaurant in Newmarket. I got £100 a week there, which was good for me. The worst-paid job was at a restaurant in Essex, where I got only £10 for a week,' said one interviewee named as Rafique. He was too ashamed to return home.

Azmal Hussain, owner of four Brick Lane restaurants, has spoken out against the exploitation and abuse of Bengali men within his industry: 'They are illegal but they are also human. Many work only to be able to eat. Who could imagine that slavery is taking place in the twenty-first century on our very doorsteps?' His support breaks the community taboo and he points out, 'I've been told not to talk about these things because of the problems it will cause to everyone.'

Mr Hussain judges it to be the lax British work permit system that enables abuse and corruption: 'I could get four work permits a year for each of my restaurants. They can be sold for £10,000 each (the going rate) on the black market – that's £160,000 a year for me.' He ruminated that, in order to free the 'curry slaves', the status of those within the country should be legalised and then new licences should be granted.

Moral and medical matters

The breaking of taboos, and the discussion of internal cultural issues in the British mainstream by south Asian migrants, has become increasingly vocal in recent years. In 2010, the Channel 4 *Dispatches* documentary *When Cousins Marry* brought the controversial issue of consanguineous marriage between first cousins to nationwide attention. A dramatic increase in cousin marriage has occurred in Britain over three decades. The majority of these marriages – over half – were between British Pakistanis. The tradition is also common within the British Bangladeshi community – almost one-quarter enter into marriage with their first cousins.

The tragic outcome of these unions is that, within a smaller gene pool, genetic mutations that are often carried as recessive genes in both spouses result in children born with birth defects and genetic disorders. British Pakistani children are ten times more likely to suffer from rare recessive genetic disorders than the general population. Children born blind, deaf, with congenital anomalies, learning difficulties, metabolic disorders, neurodegenerative conditions and skin diseases feature within the medical risks of first-cousin marriages. Infant mortality rates are higher and one-third of affected children die before they reach the age of five.

Keeping it in the family: cousins marry.

A 2000 British Childhood Visual Impairment Study Group study found that hereditary disorders accounted for one-third of severe visual impairment and blindness cases. Within the south Asian category, the Pakistani and Bangladeshi communities experienced the highest incidence: the average yearly incidence of 1.6 per 10,000 children represented an eight-fold increase in comparison with the white British population.

Many people deny the inherent danger and social cost of children born as a result of consanguineous marriage. The abuse she received for highlighting the public health issue did not deter Ann Cryer, former Labour MP for Keighley, from speaking out: 'We deal with public health issues by raising awareness, by talking about subjects such as obesity, such as drug addiction, such as alcohol.' The message was clear: consanguineous marriage should be treated no differently.

A medical research study – the Born in Bradford study – tracked 10,000 children through two decades of their lives from birth. 'Of the first 1,100 pregnant Pakistani women recruited, 70 per cent are from consanguineous marriages,' said Dr Peter Corry, a consultant paediatrician at Bradford Teaching Hospitals. The study identified nearly 150 rare genetic conditions within the city, a much greater number than to be expected within the population. Half of Bradford's children are born to Pakistani parents. The British Paediatric Surveillance Unit found that, of the 902 British children born with neurodegenerative conditions between 1997 and 2007, 8 per cent of them were from Bradford, a city home to just 1 per cent of the UK population. The number of children suffering may be small, but the disorders that they suffer can be catastrophic for them and their families. Dr Corry works with an extended family in which six children share a genetic condition that makes it unlikely they will live past their teens.

Genetic testing has been advocated for families affected by, or at risk of, genetic conditions. Dr Corry noted: 'When I came to Bradford twenty years ago, most Pakistani parents didn't understand when you were talking about genetics. But now we're seeing young Pakistani professionals with a much greater knowledge about genetic conditions.'

Although the cost to health services is high, the benefit to medicine is that families who work with genetic services assist the advancement of science. New genetic tests and treatments are found, and doctors' knowledge and insight of rare disorders increases, benefitting society as a whole.

*   *   *

Many of the first mass wave of south Asian immigrants after the Second World War envisaged their stay as temporary. They wanted to see Britain get back on its feet but they also wanted to share in the promised post-war prosperity themselves. Remember Harold Macmillan's phrase, 'You've never had it so good'?

These new Britons helped Britain become a far more prosperous and healthy country. South Asian migrants treated – and continue to treat – Britain's infirm within the NHS and private health services. What is more, they enabled Britons of all ethnicities and incomes to enjoy a better standard of living because of their revolutionary impact on the retail sector – one which increased competition, choice and efficiency of supply. Would Britain function as it does today with local grocers closing at 5 p.m. and city centre stores not opening at the weekends? The opportunities the first wave of migrants wished to export back home have instead enriched the UK both financially and culturally.

Prince William and Prince George have the diverse genetic touch that will be required to connect with and lead the Commonwealth in uncertain and changing times. The term 'Aryan' is derived from the Sanskrit word for 'noble', so it is fitting to find that, beneath the blond hair and blue eyes, they are of partial Indian descent via Princess Diana.

Six generations behind Prince William, his housekeeper foremother Eliza Kewark bore his Scottish merchant ancestor

Theodore Forbes three children. Their unmarried, long-term relationship was not unusual in their home city of Surat within the Indian state of Gujarat. One-third of British men employed in India during the late eighteenth to late nineteenth centuries took an Indian wife.

A daughter Katherine – named after Theodore's mother – was born in 1812 and settled in Scotland when she was eight years old. Her father died on their outward journey. Katherine never returned to India, but corresponded with her mother in letters written in their native tongue. Raised on the Forbes family estate in Aberdeenshire, Katherine went on to marry James Crombie, a scion of the coat manufacturing family. Their great-granddaughter Ruth Gill would take a social leap forward into the aristocracy with her 1931 marriage to Maurice Roche, 4th Baron Fermoy.

In 1954, Ruth's daughter Frances would marry Edward the Viscount Althorp (later Earl Spencer), and their daughter Lady Diana Spencer would go on to marry a prince. This is a stellar social ascent, and one that Eliza Kewark would never have imagined possible when waving off her daughter Katherine as the merchant ship SS *Blenden Hall* set sail for Britain. She herself would never visit, but her descendant will one day be King.

Chapter 6

The Chinese and Far East Asian communities

THE FASTEST-GROWING ETHNIC GROUP IN Great Britain is the Chinese community – growing 10 per cent per year, mostly due to net migration. Those who can trace some Chinese heritage now number at least a quarter of a million, but probably closer to 400,000. Compared with post-war immigration from south Asia and the West Indies, the Chinese story is smaller but they have proved to be one of the most successful groups. They have dispersed right across Britain – from Cardiff to London, Manchester to Newcastle, Nottingham to Belfast – settling in even the smallest towns and villages.

The first Chinese immigrant to be recorded in the history books is Shen Fu Tsong, a Jesuit scholar who catalogued the Bodleian Library's Chinese collection in the seventeenth century. The 21st-century Chinese community is just as scholarly. They have attained remarkable academic achievement, have one of the highest average household incomes among demographic groups in the UK, and consistently head the league tables of educational attainment.

The Chinese community is mainly concentrated in London, with Chinatown functioning as a significant cultural and employment hub, as well as one of the capital's most popular tourist attractions. Many British-Chinese citizens came to Britain from former British colonies, including Hong Kong, Malaysia, Singapore, Canada, Australia and New Zealand, so, in reality, they are the descendants of Chinese who immigrated to other countries. Those living in Britain from mainland China and Taiwan, and their descendants, represent a relatively small percentage of the British-Chinese community.

Liberalisation in China has resulted in Chinese-born citizens comprising the largest numerical group of new immigrants to the UK. In 2012, 40,000 Chinese people immigrated to Britain – the first time they have topped the league table for entry into Britain. The boom is directly associated with Chinese students entering UK universities. Five of the fastest-growing Chinese clusters are close to universities in Britain that have launched major overseas recruitment drives. While the number of Indian nationals studying in Britain has decreased, partly due to Home Office visa restrictions, Chinese educational migration grows steadily year on year. According to the Independent Schools Council's 2013 Census, the largest numbers of overseas pupils are from Hong Kong and China, with 37.1 per cent of all overseas pupils between them.

They were joined by students from Taiwan, Japan, South Korea, Malaysia and Thailand. Interestingly, Indian student numbers ranked substantially below them all, despite Prime Minister David Cameron's visits to India where he made a point of encouraging Britain's inflow of foreign tuition fees.

Children walk and play outside the Chinese Freemason Society in Limehouse in London's Docklands, 1927.

Britain boasts the oldest Chinese community in western Europe, with the first Chinese having come from Tianjin and Shanghai in the early nineteenth century. As with the west African immigrant population until the Second World War, the Chinese communities lived in and around our main ports, notably Liverpool, Cardiff and, of course, London. These communities comprised seafarers and a modest number of residents who ran shops, restaurants and boarding houses. Limehouse, in the East End of London, was the capital's epicentre for the Chinese community. It was originally established by the East India Company, which was accumulating immense wealth from importing popular Chinese commodities such as tea, ceramics and silks. Most large cities now boast a thriving Chinatown – Manchester, Liverpool, Birmingham, Glasgow and even Aberdeen.

John Anthony, a Chinese sailor, was the pioneer who provided accommodation for visiting Chinese seamen in the late eighteenth century. He was so successful, and his contribution to Britain was so great, that a special Act of Parliament was passed in 1805 to make him a British citizen. What extraordinary influence – not many immigrants can match this feat.

The big surge in numbers took place in the 1950s, when a new wave of immigrants from Hong Kong came to live in the UK. This was the group that opened the restaurants and takeaways across the length and breadth of Britain. The Chinese began to be joined by increasing numbers of economic migrants from Malaysia and Singapore in the 1960s and '70s, some of whom first came here as students. The first of many Chinese students to graduate from a British university was Wong Fun, who received his MD in 1855 from Edinburgh.

The wave of immigration from Hong Kong started to slow in the 1980s, when rising living standards and rapid urbanisation in Hong Kong, Singapore and Malaysia quelled the urge to move abroad. However, this decline was countered by a rise in the number of students and skilled emigrants from the People's Republic of China, particularly from the north east of the country.

Mike Bloomberg, the former mayor of New York City, argues that it is vital for Britain to keep its doors open to inward migration. Based on his own experience of running America's most vibrant city, he contends that new arrivals gave the Big Apple a vital competitive advantage. Bloomberg believes Britain should have invited far more Hong Kong Chinese to settle in the UK when China took over in the 1990s. In Bloomberg's view, major cities need immigrants to keep their economies internationally competitive. Bloomberg, who has amassed a fortune of £33 billion and is a leading philanthropist, judges immigrants to be capable of challenging the resident population and injecting entrepreneurial verve: 'We definitely need immigrants. That's exactly true for London and the UK in particular. I thought when Hong Kong went back to the Chinese, England should have opened its borders.'

Certainly, it is now the case that some Chinese multi-billionaires rival the Russians in terms of sheer wealth. Like their Russian contemporaries, they own a cluster of homes worldwide. Joseph Lau is one of them. He made his fortune in Hong Kong as a high-profile corporate raider. In 2012, he donated £6 million to King's College London to pursue research on Chinese issues.

Case study: Olivia Yin

A lady marching to her own tune

Olivia Yin is a confident, free-spirited and visionary woman. She was born into a privileged military family which served the revolutionary Red Army during communism and has since prospered greatly via capitalist enterprise. Her roots are in Chengdu, the provincial capital of south-west China's Sichuan province. She became a British citizen in 2012 after a residency of eleven years.

Olivia was ahead of the current private schooling trend, which illustrates that almost 40 per cent of the current 25,000 independent school students whose parents live overseas hail from Hong Kong (19.3 per cent) and mainland China (18 per cent). They occupy more desks in British schools than students from the whole of the remainder of Europe. She is the perfect example of the educational migrants from mainland China who flock to the UK lured by the characteristics and kudos of our education system and exceptional institutions.

She says that, in 2001,

> 60 per cent of my classmates had left the country to study
> abroad at that time. I think I was the first one to go to the
> UK. For most of them it was easier to go to Canada or
> Australia or the US because it's much cheaper there and a
> much easier process.

Her experience as an A-level student at Hurtwood House,
a leading co-educational boarding school set in 200 acres of
the Surrey Hills, was radically different to her education in
China and extremely refreshing. She also felt very welcome
and accepted by her teachers and classmates. Nowadays, 10
per cent of Hurtwood House's intake comes from the upper
echelons of Chinese society, where annual fees of £38,220
and a distance of almost 6,000 miles are no barriers to entry.
Indeed, 80 per cent of wealthy Chinese students are sent
abroad for their education, according to Rupert Hoogew-
erf, publisher of the Hurun Report and the China Rich List.
His most recent annual survey of China's top entrepreneurs
and investors reports that 29 per cent of participants found
the UK to be the ideal country for their children to receive
a secondary education, while 26 per cent favoured the US.
The tidal wave of private school fees is a great liquid boost to
the national coffers.

Olivia learned English as a foreign language, but she was
miles ahead in maths and science. It is easy to see why she

had an academic advantage and why many Chinese students prefer to study overseas:

> I don't necessarily agree with the education system there, it is very good at the foundation when you go to primary school, but afterwards the level of work is just *too* much. We are in the class from 7.30 a.m. until twelve o'clock and every lesson is fifty minutes long. You have a ten-minute break between each lesson. There are five lessons in the morning, then a 1.5-/2-hour break. Then lessons until 5 p.m. followed by evening classes 7–9 p.m.

At Hurtwood House, evening preparation time was normal, but in China this time was used for additional learning and examinations, and homework was given after the session:

> I was lucky to sleep at 11 p.m; 12 p.m.–1 a.m. is the norm when work is finished. The regimen doesn't give much time for sleep, creativity or self-development. You don't have much time for yourself, you don't understand yourself, you don't learn much about life, you don't think about yourself as a person; how you want to develop. You just do all of the work that they give you, which is compulsory work. It really kills the imagination and creativity.

Olivia's belief in the stimulation of imagination and creativity that a UK education provides Far East Asian students is borne out in the burgeoning careers and successful London Fashion Week collections of the Taiwanese designers Shao Yen Chen and Niza Huang, who, respectively, studied fashion design & knitwear at Central St Martin's and jewellery & metalwork at Sheffield University in the past decade.

Beauty, intelligence and wealth are salves that have eased many exceptional foreign women into British society. Olivia has found the workplace as welcoming as her places of study, but has heard from other students, 'especially the boys', that racism can be a common experience for mainland Chinese migrants. She has, however, experienced the rudeness of London's black cab drivers. In China, modesty and politeness are socially ingrained and expected virtues. Olivia was raised to treat everyone from family elders to household staff with the utmost respect, so the frequent rudeness of rogue cabbies is a particular culture shock:

> I don't think it is for the foreign people, I just think that they are rude in general, so I just decided that I am going to drive myself ... black cabs are one of the most expensive taxis in the world but they make you feel like you are begging them to take a ride.

Olivia is uncharacteristically bold within her culture and likes to do things her own way. She is immensely intelligent, incredibly cultured and exquisitely polished, like an iron fist in a bespoke fur-lined satin glove. Her sense of style has served her well after visa regulations did not afford her the smooth segue into business consultancy after university. 'I understand because the unemployment rate is high here, so the government does not give much working visas for graduates.'

Luckily, prior to Olivia's graduation, the International Graduates Scheme (IGS) was launched. It allowed non-European Economic Area nationals such as herself – who had successfully completed a UK degree or post-graduate qualification – to work or start up their own business without requiring a work permit. The IGS ran for one year before being replaced by Tier 1 (Post Study Work).

> I feel it was quite an inadequate system as you had a one-year working visa but you couldn't apply before your current visa ran out. By the time you get the working visa, there are only ten months left. You couldn't possibly apply for a graduate scheme if you only had ten months left and you usually apply for the schemes one year before. Everything was too late for applying to a graduate scheme or getting a proper job in a company.

As is the case in many successful migrant stories, tenacity and inspiration led towards self-empowerment and entrepreneurship. Having observed her family's good codes of conduct and adept management of people and resources, Olivia easily transferred her skills and education to the commercial world: 'I learned when I was young from watching them, so decided to go into business myself.'

Olivia found great opportunities in areas where many graduates actively seek work. Her unique and opulent style – G London jewels, Dior handbags, Louboutin shoes, Chanel and Alexander McQueen for daywear and the occasional touch of mink – attracted the admiration and inquisition of visiting Chinese nationals:

> When I shopped on Bond Street three or four years ago, the rich Chinese people started to do private shopping tours instead of coach tours. Their English might not be good to communicate with the shop assistants – they like to see Chinese people in the shops that they can talk to, so I got lots of clients that way.

Her lucrative freelance opportunity evolved into lifestyle consultancy: 'More and more people want to send their children here. In my time, people sent their children to school here, but now they want to live here and be a part of society.' Olivia assisted her clients' smooth transitions and integration into London's elite environs and high society by advising them on major life decisions and setting the cornerstones of the foundation of a new life in a vastly different culture:

> I tell them where to buy the house, which school to go to, and compare the pros and cons and introduce them to the right people to meet, to the right functions, to the right events they need to go. Just like the things they do in China

except when they come here they don't know where to start. As I've been in London so long I have many connections, which I have used to build a business.

Apart from language barriers for some Chinese newcomers, which are overcome with the employment of translators and language tutors, her high net-worth clients have had few problems easing themselves into London's elite networks. Olivia retains her regional Mandarin accent but speaks English with the ease and eloquence of her mother tongue: 'I think the English society is quite welcoming to foreigners.' Indeed.

In 2013, Olivia consulted with Bicester Village on strategies to increase the number of lucrative Chinese shopping tourists, and she used her cultural insight to improve their shopping experiences. Many economic sectors gain from high-spending Chinese tourists, including luxury retail, hotels, theatres and restaurants.

But would the UK and US be able to cope if looser Chinese policy directed 1.2 billion tourists straight to our shores? The UK has a long-standing Chinese community, hailing from the former British colony of Hong Kong. Olivia asserts that the new high net-worth Chinese migrants do not tend to mix with the pre-existing community, who mainly migrated away from poverty in search of work overseas. 'They speak in Cantonese, which is more difficult than speaking English to us.' Many Cantonese migrants worked very hard over several decades to afford to purchase their own homes in the major cities and small towns of the UK. One thing they have in common with the new mainland arrivals is a cultural and economic attachment to bricks and mortar.

Olivia has great insight into the current boom in mainland Chinese property buyers, who in 2013 accounted for 4.2 per cent of prime London sales – up 2 per cent on the previous year. Property agent Knight Frank now ranks them fourth, after the Indians, Russians and French, within London's high-end housing market. 'Chinese people like to invest in property, I have a friend who is only twenty-three and hasn't even finished her master's yet, she has a whole property portfolio in north England.' The student's family fund afforded her this speculative opportunity. 'We don't only buy property to live in, we buy property to invest because in the Chinese mind, property investment is the safest and also, in the UK, the price has never gone down. We bring a lot of money into the UK.'

It seems that the pursuit of happiness, and the personal fulfilment gained via a rich quality of life and high standard of living, motivates and retains migrants of exceptional independent means to live, work and play in the UK. They are freer of spirit and less restricted in following business paths divergent from the conservative norm in their homelands. Olivia agrees:

> People here are always looking for opportunities to improve their life. In China, people are very settled and they know their business and they are quite happy with it. In China they do not talk about politics or the world situation as it is

seen as nothing to do with them. I don't think they are really involved in the whole society; they are very much involved in their own family life.

Olivia enjoys pushing the boundaries of herself and her home culture. She prefers curiosity to insularity, questioning to ignoring, and discussing to disconnecting. She relishes literature and global current affairs as well as champagne and couture fashion. Her family would like to see her settled and they have offered to buy her a house, but she prefers to rent and go with the flow of life, which is against the grain of her native culture.

Asked if she would ever make a permanent return to China, Olivia sniffs at China's high pollution levels and smiles at the ease of basing herself in the UK for convenient trips to mainland Europe. She cites two main reasons why she would prefer to remain in the UK:

> First, the political situation is quite difficult [in China], and second, I am used to living here. The lifestyle is completely different. What people do in China is different than what people do here. I enjoy going out to the theatre, to all the concerts, to the events, to cocktails, but in China people just don't do this. They play *mah jong*, from my cousins up to my grandmother. I'd rather have afternoon tea with my friend and talk about life rather than just playing the game.

*   *   *

The Chinese community in the capital is particularly buoyant. There are Chinese community centres in Chinatown, Barnet, Camden, Hackney, Islington, Lambeth, Haringey and Tower Hamlets, where children can attend class at weekends and learn about their traditional culture. The Charing Cross Library, supported by Westminster City Council, boasts the largest collection of Chinese books, CDs and videos in any UK public library. Meanwhile, the Chinese immigrant community also support organisations such as the London Chinatown Chinese Association.

Chinese immigrants have faced a number of hardships and problems. For the older generation, language remains a problem and this inability to converse has led to medical problems associated with isolation and depression. Some have also had problems finding accommodation, since this was previously provided by an employer (more often than not, a restaurant). This has led to Chinese community groups launching advocacy and counselling services. Those working in the restaurant trade, particularly men, can be tempted to spend time late at night in gambling clubs – the perennial vice of the Chinese community worldwide. One recalls that Lee Kuan Yew made gambling illegal even in Singapore – a sanction that was only lifted in 2011.

Over the last decade there has been an alarming surge in the incidence of illegal human trafficking by international criminal gangs. These shady characters have brought large numbers (no one knows the precise number) of unskilled Chinese migrants into the country to undertake a range of grisly jobs as well as work as prostitutes. The Morecambe Bay tragedy of February 2004, when twenty-three Chinese cockle pickers drowned as they were trapped by incoming tides, revealed just how prevalent this illicit trade in human trafficking had become. These unfortunate souls were paid a paltry £5 for every 25 kilograms of cockles they collected from the shore of Morecambe Bay. Superintendent Mick Gradwell, the Lancashire Constabulary police detective who led the investigation following the tragedy, reckons criminal gangs were funnelling as much as £1 million per day to China by exploiting workers all around England. He points out that 'tens of thousands of illegal Chinese workers were living in the country, building up hidden communities and building a life below official recognition.' As the victims had all been illegal immigrants, their families in the Fujian province were not entitled to financial compensation. In February 2014, ten years after the tragedy occurred, Triad boss Lin Liang Ren was released from prison halfway through his fourteen-year manslaughter sentence – equating to four months served for the death of each victim. He was deported to China.

Research recently undertaken by Professor Gary Craig and his academic team at Durham University have found evidence that the numbers of people trafficked for labour exploitation may soon exceed those brought into the UK for sexual exploitation. 'The research that I've done with colleagues suggests there may be upwards of 10,000 people at any one time in the UK in conditions which we would class as modern slavery,' says Craig. The professor argues that there is a 'real problem' getting people to acknowledge that 'slavery exists in the UK'.

The Vietnamese story: great hardship and some success

According to the 2001 Census, there were 22,954 Vietnamese-born people in England and Wales. However, these figures need to be treated with caution since there is no explicit Vietnamese category. There is no information about Vietnamese people born in Britain, although community organisations estimated in 2007 that there are at least 55,000 Vietnamese in England and Wales, 20,000 of whom are undocumented migrants and around 5,000 overseas students.

The Vietnamese who arrived in Britain after the long-running Vietnamese conflict of the 1960s and '70s had gone through a living hell. Recounting their story, Ian Burrell pointed out in *The Independent* that they were 'driven from their homes in Vietnam by war and ethnic cleansing, they risked drowning and piracy by fleeing to the seas in thousands of tiny craft'. Meanwhile, 'those that reached Hong Kong were herded into refugee camps where they remained for years'. They were the refugees the world ignored.

Following the US–Vietnamese War, a mere 300 were granted leave to remain in Britain in 1975. Only three were given asylum the subsequent year. Britain took a closer interest after China invaded Vietnam in the late 1970s as a result of a border dispute. This sparked an exodus of ethnic Chinese-Vietnamese citizens from North Vietnam, with many of these refugees taking to boats in an attempt to reach Hong Kong. Most of these refugees were poor farmers and fishermen from rural areas. If they managed to make it to Hong Kong, they remained there for years in miserable transit camps.

A total of 11,450 asylum seekers arrived in Britain from Hong Kong's refugee camps, in two quotas. Another 3,150 refugees were rescued at sea and, later on, a programme of family reunion brought 3,850 Vietnamese to Britain. South-east Asian refugees made up a tiny minority of Britain's overall asylum intake between 1975 and 1990; only 1.1 per cent of those seeking asylum from the region were granted leave to remain in Britain. The Vietnamese who came to Britain from Hong Kong were housed in former army camps and then deliberately located in towns and villages all across Britain in a 'dispersal' housing programme. This proved to be a huge mistake because the Vietnamese refugees were unable to communicate with the locals. What is more, they could not buy the foodstuffs they were familiar with. At the time, some Scottish towns – such as Cumbernauld – did not even sell rice in the local shops. This only compounded the refugees' sense of isolation and led to considerable distress and a feeling of marginalisation.

The Vietnamese refugee programme proved to be the pilot for compulsory dispersion operations in the UK. The government strategically spread refugees out in cities across the UK in an effort to lessen the financial and social costs of resettlement, while simultaneously averting political backlash and cultural clash. Micro-dispersions – some as small as four families in one cluster – were aimed at minimising public resentment of these refugees, but it actually made their integration into British society harder, and increased their feeling of cultural isolation. The Vietnamese found themselves in a country in which there was no previously established ethnic community they could join, as was the case with the east Asians forced to flee Uganda.

Many of the refugees were illiterate in Vietnamese, let alone English. The government's strategy aimed at avoiding 'ghetto-isation' proved to be an abject failure. Immigrants draw comfort from the ghetto, particularly when they first arrive in a foreign country.

Over time, the Vietnamese marched with their feet: they fled windswept Cumbernauld, and the other towns where the authorities had dumped them, and they clustered in major conurbations such as Manchester, Birmingham and, particularly, London – where there were thriving Chinese communities, and shops in which they could buy familiar food. The figures speak for themselves: of the 2,000 Vietnamese who went to Scotland, barely a couple of hundred remained to ponder how to vote in the Scottish referendum.

Ian Burrell pointed out in 2000 that more than half the Vietnamese migrants to Britain were unemployed, half their adult community could still not speak English, and many of their families were living in chronic poverty. Worse still, 'at least 400 Vietnamese in London are having treatment for addiction to heroin or crack cocaine, and mental illness is running at double the national average'. Burrell quotes Vi Tran, a senior drug worker at An-Viet, a Vietnamese refugee group based in Hackney, who observed: 'There are very serious problems in the community. Adult Vietnamese who have not been educated here have little chance of work and are being struck down by drugs, mental health problems and gambling.'

Long-term unemployment and the inability to fit in led to crime. Police were concerned at the growing incidence of organised crime, with Vietnamese gangs – modelled on the Chinese Triads – linked to a series of violent attacks, including a murder in south-east London. As is so often the case, Vietnamese boat people came to Britain for a new life but found unemployment and despair.

Britain's criterion for asylum was not as stringent as that of Australia and the US, where Vietnamese refugees of higher educational standards and English language proficiency found it easier to establish themselves, and prospered accordingly. Now that more than half of Britain's Vietnamese community resides in London – with high concentrations in the boroughs of Hackney, Greenwich and Lewisham – they are experiencing much more successful outcomes than the first generation of migrants.

In recent years, the Vietnamese community has begun to put down roots and prosper, mainly as a result of education. As they became more established, they have launched new businesses – particularly restaurants, grocery stores, travel agents and entertainment venues. Parts of Hackney are now dominated by thriving Vietnamese enterprises, not least on the Kingsland Road or the 'Pho Mile', as it has become affectionately known to Londoners. Indeed, the southern end of Kingsland Road is home to twenty Vietnamese restaurants that attract a hip crowd. When Russell Brand turns up at your restaurants – as he does – you know you have become part of the British establishment.

The Vietnamese who settled in the capital originally, moved to some of the most notorious estates in North Peckham – notably the Kidbrooke and the Pepys. I wonder what Pepys would have to say – or write in his diary – about that. However, through hard work and education, many in the community have dragged themselves off the bottom and begun to make a new life for themselves. Extended families have joined them from their old home country, and their children, educated in Britain and fluent in English, have seized the opportunities they were offered by their new home country. Within the London borough of Lambeth, Vietnamese pupils – along with Indian and Chinese pupils – achieved higher results than other ethnic groups in the borough.

As Jessica Mai Sims writes in *The Vietnamese Community in Britain: Thirty Years On*: 'Education is said to be highly prized among the Vietnamese community, not only because it forms the basis for all learning, but it also promotes the cultivation of spiritual and personal worth.' Ms Sims points out that education is perceived as the primary marker of social mobility since it provides individuals with the skills 'to communicate, relate and adapt to society, and qualify for employment'.

Of course, there is something else rather trendy firmly associated with the Vietnamese: they have brought us power dressing for the fingernails. In the last decade, the nail industry has become the fastest-growing UK Vietnamese business sector, accounting for over half of all Vietnamese businesses in London and listed as the largest employer of Vietnamese. Nail salons were an idea imported from America and they thrived as a result of transnational family networks.

Alarmingly, some Vietnamese migrants now arrive as slaves trafficked by criminal gangs whose profits are second only to drug barons in the world of international organised crime. In 2013, the *Sunday Times* launched a campaign to bring the issue of Britain's modern-day slavery to public attention, asking: 'Who's really paying for your manicure?' The newspaper found that many of the women servicing the cities' New York-style boom in high-maintenance manicures had been lured to Britain to fill lucrative jobs that didn't exist. They had been forced to lacquer nails by day and serve as prostitutes at night. The 'Britain's Hidden Slaves' campaign also brought attention to the plight of children trafficked from Vietnam and forced to cultivate cannabis.

The Malaysian community

According to the 2001 Census, there were over 49,000 people born in Malaysia who were living in England and Wales – an increase of almost 6,000 on the figure a decade previously. The total is now over 63,000.

Many of them are ethnic Chinese, whose ancestors settled in Malaysia in five historic waves. The first wave arrived during the early fifteenth-century Malacca empire. The fifth wave comprised of a small number of citizens from the People's Republic of China, who arrived the 1990s. The majority of these migrants were the foreign spouses of Malaysians or coaches of national sports.

Regardless of ethnic origin, Malaysian migrants to the UK tend to live in the same cities and neighbourhoods as Chinese immigrants from Hong Kong and mainland China. Most Malaysians live in the capital, but there are communities in Portsmouth, Sheffield, Leeds and neighbourhoods in and around Manchester.

Britain enjoys strong educational links with Malaysia. Universities such as Nottingham have established campuses in the country, while UK independent schools such as Epsom College have also established satellite schools in Kuala Lumpur,

Malaysia. In 2013, there were 14,500 Malaysians studying at a tertiary level in the United Kingdom, making Malaysians one of the largest overseas student groups in Britain. The Chartered Institute of Marketing has built up a particularly strong relationship with Malaysian students and now has international offices in Malaysia as well as Hong Kong and Singapore.

Malaysians are big shoppers in Britain. Malaysian-born Jimmy Choo, the women's shoe designer, has been based in the UK for all his adult life, having been at the Cordwainers' Technical College in Hackney – now an integral part of the London College of Fashion. How many social security benefits for the English have been paid for from the taxes on the Choo shoe sales he has inspired worldwide? Designer goods tend to attract a hefty sales tax in the Far East, so visitors from Malaysia, Thailand and, particularly, China are growing fast and spending big.

Both the Malaysian and Singaporean economies are currently booming, with economic growth rates far above those achieved in western Europe. This has enabled many of their citizens to invest in London property. Indeed, the pages of the *Straits Times* – Singapore's most popular newspaper – and other leading publications feature advertisements for properties in Britain's capital every day.

According to the property agent Jones Lang & Wootton, Malaysians buy nearly as much of the capital's newly built housing stock at the higher end of the price range as

local buyers. Not least apartments within One Hyde Park –
London's most expensive residential development.

Not forgetting Singapore...

While it is a small city state with a population of 5.4 million,
Singapore is an important export market for Britain. Indeed,
it is the UK's largest trading partner in south-east Asia, with
two-thirds of UK exports to this region flowing into Singapore.

Singapore is a thriving commercial centre, ranking as the
world's fourth-biggest financial centre and the fifth-busiest
port. At the same time, Britain attracts over two-thirds of all
Singaporean investment into the European Union, boasting
a cumulative stock of £20.6 billion, with financial/insurance
services, real estate and ICT being the most significant sectors.

Education links between Singapore and the United Kingdom are strong. As of 2011, more than 3,000 Singaporeans were
studying in the United Kingdom. Some leading institutions,
such as the LSE, have forged a long-standing relationship with
Singapore. The British Council estimates that around 80,000
UK qualifications are awarded annually in Singapore. These
cultural and educational ties have been to the great advantage
of Britain as well as Singapore, and it is a foundation upon
which we need to build in the future.

* * *

Far East Asian immigrants to the United Kingdom may be attracted by the quality of our lives and education, but they have added quality to our lives in turn, educating us with their cultures and habits. Britain's relationship with the Far East Asian nations during previous centuries and in colonisation may be unacknowledged, or even unknown to many, but few Britons will ever forget the location of their regional Chinatown.

Leicester-born national television treasure Gok Wan – whose mother is white English and father is Hong Kong-born Chinese – is readily welcomed into the closets and bra cups of a generation of British women to whom he has granted a fairy godfather-like *Fashion Fix*. In time, the 'otherness' – a fact or feeling of being different, which Gok and many other Britons of sole or mixed Far East Asian descent (and those from other BME ethnicities too) have felt – could dissipate into a condition of 'Britishness', seen either by the eye meeting its own gaze in the mirror or the eye of a white English beholder.

Many British citizens of sole Far East Asian lineage have never visited their ancestral countries, don't speak their indigenous languages and are well adjusted to having a dual cultural identity. Fair beauties beheld by the world as icons of English femininity and style include Alexa Chung, whose surname – and hence father – is Chinese. She sets global trends as an iconic UK beauty and also contributes to British *Vogue* magazine. Similarly, English rose Kate Beckinsale says of her

eyes that the 'slightly almond shape is a legacy of my Bur-
mese great-grandfather'. Iain Duncan Smith, Leader of the
Conservative Party between 2001 and 2003 and currently
Secretary of State for Work and Pensions, may not be quite
as photogenic as Alexa or Kate, but he shares their Far East
Asian heritage – his great-grandmother was Japanese. What
he did not physically inherit from his Samurai ancestors he
surely inherited in terms of class: the Samurai were always
closely associated with the middle and upper echelons of
their society.

Chapter 7

The Middle Eastern community

IN MY BOOK AT LEAST, the Arabs and the Jews must share the same chapter. In London, the least discriminating and most multicultural city on Earth, Arabs, Jews, Sunnis, Shias are all equally welcome, and they should remain so – as long as they leave their multiple, interminable, and culturally addictive disputes behind them. It seems to me that the unremitting killing of their neighbours' children sits uneasily with a predilection for the persecution narrative, whoever is carrying that out. Indeed, several cultural norms rooted in that region seem to me little more acceptable than the FGM discussed earlier

– I would, for example, cite the tendency towards state- and religion-backed misogyny. However, free from their ancestral home affairs, Britain's own Middle Eastern population is undoubtedly ethnically diverse, well established, and long under-recorded.

Unsurprisingly, some of our hard-won freedoms appear to have a great value and appeal to many from such a dysfunctional region. Several pan-Arabian international newspapers are headquartered in the UK, including the rival daily broadsheets *Al-Hayat* and *Asharq Al-Awsat*. The *Maghreb Review* was founded by Algerian Mohamed Ben-Madani in 1976 and its views have been much sought-after since the Arab Spring. In addition, the Arabic news channel Al Jazeera is transmitted to most British homes and the BBC also broadcasts BBC Arabic from London's Broadcasting House. Arsenal, one of Britain's most prominent football clubs, plays at the Emirates Stadium, and over a quarter of Sainsbury's is owned by Qatar Holding – the global investment house established by the Qatar Investment Authority in 2006. Despite the Arab prominence within the UK, many Britons have limited experience of, or no interaction whatsoever with, the UK's Middle Eastern community.

The Middle Eastern community is highly visible, distinctly audible and fragrant too. The supercars of Knightsbridge bearing Arabic licence plates – creating many sleepless nights for local residents – herald the beginning of the Arab Summer. North African or Lebanese *shaabi* pop music is as much an accompaniment to *shawarma* kebabs and falafel, as salad and humus are in some west London takeaways. Londoners with super-refined noses are able to discern whether the veiled ladies wafting by hail from Oman, Saudi Arabia or the Sudan by the aroma of their frankincense perfume.

London has always absorbed the most migrants, and the Middle Eastern communities are no exception. The majority of Middle Eastern migrants choose to live in the capital and have carved distinct niches throughout the city. The Arab community is most notable in the wealthy enclaves of SW1. The fact that the borough of Westminster houses the capital's highest density of Arabic speakers is evident from the dominant businesses on the Edgware Road and the residents around Park Lane. The biggest buyers of prime London real estate – the £30 million stucco confections of Belgravia and Holland Park, and the super-secure £100 million residences of Chelsea and Regent's Park – are mainly Arab, particularly Saudi. The properties are usually only occupied during the summer season. A palatial Hyde Park home with parking space for thirty cars was bought by a Saudi princess in 2010. In 2011, it remained unoccupied by the princess, but fully staffed and filled with fresh flowers in case of her arrival.

The Bishops Avenue, Hampstead, known as London's 'Billionaires' Row', appears to have hit the skids in recent years. A number of houses purchased by the Saudi royal family in the 1990s have never been lived in and were left to the elements, although some have more recently been sold on.

That is the extreme. By considerable contrast, the north

African community within Kensington and Chelsea fills a lower socio-economic strata than that of the Arabian diaspora. Many of the estimated 8,000 Moroccans resident in the community's main UK hub of North Kensington migrated in the 1960s. They were recruited to positions in the hotel and catering industries alongside workers from Palestine. Ladbroke Grove is home to a distinctive Moroccan community – the Golborne Road vicinity is often referred to as 'Little Morocco' due to the percentage of Moroccan restaurants and shops, and the Maghrebian fare sits and sells well alongside Portuguese cuisine. Outside of the capital, Trowbridge in Wiltshire is home to the UK's largest Moroccan population.

The experience of Middle Eastern migrants in Hull – mainly Iraqi Kurds and Afghanis – is notable. In 2001, the Humberside city appeared to be one of the least ethnically diverse large British cities – 749 Chinese residents accounted for the largest non-white population out of its 243,589 inhabitants. In 2011, the growth of the city's Middle Eastern community led to some locals nicknaming the HU3 postal area 'Springbankistan'.

Hull welcomed its first Middle Eastern refugee in 1999, when Iraqi Kurds were dispersed throughout Britain in a government strategy to spread asylum seekers nationwide. More Iraqi Kurds arrived in later years and suffered from culture shock and minor discord in their host city. Asylum seeker Karwan Ali recalls: 'Our young men can sleep all together in a double bed, but in England they call it gay doing that. When English people see that, they think all Kurdish people are gay, but it's not true!'

Cultural distrust rose after the 9/11 attacks in 2001 and Britain's 2003 war with Iraq – local discord with their new neighbours was heightened during these emotional and combative periods.

Operation Haven: the Royal Marines commanded a humanitarian effort to rescue Kurdish refugees on the Iraq/Turkish border in 1991.

The Kurds have sought asylum in the UK since the 1980s, when their culture and lives came under attack in Turkey, Iraq and, to some extent, Iran. Kurds in Turkey were forced to assimilate into the Turkish culture. In 1991, the Kurdish language was banned and it became a criminal offence to publish Kurdish newspapers or books. The Refugee Council states that, of over 12,500 asylum applications made by Turkish nationals between 1980 and 1993, the majority were Kurdish. Most who were granted asylum settled within the London boroughs of Hackney and Haringey. Their reception was not viewed as warm. The British government did not establish a resettlement programme for the Kurds, nor did it seek to help local authorities finance their settlement.

Turkish Kurds lived alongside an established Turkish community that had been resident in London since the military coups of the 1970s and '80s. The strong community associations the Turkish Cypriot community had established were utilised by the incoming Kurds, who also found an economic fit within the Turkish Cypriot clothing and catering industries.

More ethnic Kurds arrived from Iraq after Saddam Hussein launched the Al-Anfal Campaign, which utilised mass executions and chemical attacks on Kurdish towns in an attempt to purge them from the Arab population. If only a separate nation state of Kurdistan had been created when the Ottoman empire and Persia were divided after the First World War, then perhaps, with an acknowledged homeland, regional stability may have been assured and many lives saved.

Shortly after their arrival, they managed an effective campaign against their deportation with the support of London's existing Turkish community.

* * *

Middle Eastern migration is not the new phenomenon that most might think. The presence of Arabs, Jews, Persians and Turks in Britain is not always motivated by politics. Economics forms the basis of many settlement waves. Middle Eastern ethnicities settled in Britain long before Yemeni seamen established themselves in British dock cities – including Cardiff, Liverpool and London – in the nineteenth century. Their roots are strong and deep within British soil.

Cornish and Wiltshire soil have yielded north African coins from Carthage and Numidia in the third and second centuries BC. The ancient Phoenicians – inhabitants of modern Lebanon's coast and Syria's Tartus Governorate – arrived on these shores as traders prior to the Roman invasion. They had a particular interest in the tin deposits of the British Isles and closely guarded the location of Cornish tin mines, which allowed them to trade and market the metal for optimal profit.

Medieval texts during the time of the Christian crusades, such as the fourteenth-century Guy of Warwick romance, referred to the Arabs and Saracens in an 'otherness' context. They were portrayed as the antithesis of the Christian West in terms of race, religion and culture.

African-American actor Ira Aldridge portraying Othello in William
Mulready's 1800s portrait.

Under the pen of William Shakespeare, the PR profile of
Arabs – represented by the black Moor Othello – changed

dramatically. Shakespeare is said to have been inspired by Abd el-Ouahed ben Messaoud ben Mohammed Anoun, but Othello's notably sub-Saharan physiognomy appears to refute this. History is always stronger than fiction and Anoun, the Moorish ambassador to the court of Queen Elizabeth I in 1600, is a great representative of early Arab migrants to Britain. As principal secretary to the Sultan of Morocco, Ahmad I al-Mansur, Anoun spent six months in England to promote the establishment of an Anglo–Moroccan alliance against Spain.

Ever since she was excommunicated by Pope Pius V in 1570, Queen Elizabeth I had been keen to build up trading links with the Ottoman empire and the Barbary rulers of the Maghreb. In 1579, the Ottoman Sultan wrote a carefully worded letter to the Queen of England promising safe passage by land and sea to English traders and English merchant ships across the Ottoman territories. With the removal of papal levies for trading with the infidels, the English were keen to extend their reach on a global scale. Both the Ottoman empire and Barbary monarch offered potential alliances against the Catholic powers on the continent – principally Spain and France, who had proved hostile to the British sovereign. No wonder, then, that it was the first Queen Elizabeth's reign in which the East India Company was created and prospered. Britain went global in an Elizabethan frenzy of enterprise.

Although Queen Elizabeth I declined the Moroccan ambassador's request for an English fleet to assist a Moroccan invasion of Spain, she did welcome him to her court – it was also a useful alliance for the English monarchy. Elizabeth I accepted commercial agreements with Morocco and continued to discuss the possibility of joint military operations.

* * *

Although currently smaller than most other British Muslim communities, Britain's Yemeni citizens were the first Muslim group to have been established in the country. Yemeni sailors primarily settled in Britain's dock cities – around 1,500 lived in Cardiff during the 1920s and comprised 50 per cent of the city's ethnic minority population. Most of Liverpool's Arab community is of Yemeni origin – descendants of the seamen who settled in the city during the early 1900s. Around 400 Liverpudlian newsagents are estimated to be Yemeni-owned.

Early twentieth-century Yemeni migrants were single men who took up trades away from the docklands within the industrial towns and cities including Manchester, Middlesbrough, Sheffield and Swansea. Though sharing a Yemeni nationality, speaking the same language and practising the same religion, the migrants identified themselves as members of a tribal group – hailing from either North Yemen or South Yemen – as the regions were separate nations until the unification of 1990. Until 1941 (and Sheikh Muhammad Qassim al'Alawi's establishment of the Edward Street *zawiya* prayer centre – Birmingham's first mosque), Yemeni migrants had few forums in which to practise their Muslim faith. Some married local white British women and began to lose their cultural roots; others remain single and observant of their faith to this day.

British-Yemeni boxers Khalid Yafai – the first Briton to win the Under-17 World Championships – and Naseem Hamed were born to Yemeni parents in Birmingham and Sheffield respectively. Many Yemenis worked in the Birmingham metal-forming trades and returned to Yemen when the industry fell into decline, although in 2001, Yemenis were estimated to comprise around 1 per cent of Birmingham's population.

Although Yemeni migration predates that of the post-Second World War Commonwealth wave, the community has been an 'invisible minority' within the British consciousness. The 1990s saw the emergence of Yemeni organisations including the Yemeni Development Foundation and the Yemeni Women's Association, which have sought to support the UK's Yemeni community and increase its social recognition.

In 2010, 200 Yemeni Jews escaped persecution in the northern town of Raida and were granted secret asylum in the UK on the basis that they had relatives within the country. British-Yemeni Jews had complained about the regular denials of visas for their relatives who were living under Yemeni government protection and demanded they should be afforded refugee status. Some of the complainants had settled in Britain after their expulsion from Arab and Muslim countries during the 1948 Arab–Israeli War. Their own past experiences, or cultural memory of anti-Semitism and political instability, galvanised them to aid their persecuted kin.

'The UK will allow the Raida Jews with UK ties to leave, but it's important that they don't officially leave the country as refugees,' a government source said at the time. Upon their arrival in the UK, the political migrants were absorbed by their families, who were settled and economically established within north-west and east London's Jewish enclaves and cosmopolitan circles.

Due to their cultural affinity with the Stamford Hill Charedi (ultra orthodox) Jewish community, most Yemeni Jews have settled in their vicinity. Charedi Jews, whose origins are in central Europe, have embraced their Yemeni kin by sponsoring asylum applications and adopting their children. These newcomers do well and have several successful role models to aspire to, including the sensually bohemian interior decorator Sera Hersham-Loftus. Her trademark style channels the 'desert tribe' philosophy and aesthetic, which enables the creation of a comforting home wherever she or her famous clients – including the stellar Primrose Hill set – may go.

Many Britons assume that Middle Eastern migrants will follow the Muslim religion. As the Yemeni Jews illustrate, this is not necessarily the case. Some of Britain's most prominent and pillar-of-the-establishment migrants hail from a Middle Eastern/Jewish lineage: the Thatcherite Saatchi brothers Charles and Maurice were born in 1940s Baghdad. Their family fled to Britain from Iraq – as religious persecution took hold – and established a prosperous business based on the acquisition of two north London textile mills. The Saatchi brothers, whose surname translates as 'watchmaker' in Persian and Iraqi Arabic, showed their good timing in the 1980s, when they founded the world's largest and most iconic advertising agency – Saatchi & Saatchi. Their current advertising concern – M&C Saatchi (founded in 1995) – is listed on the London Stock Exchange.

Keep it brotherly: the Saatchi brothers have maintained a strong business partnership and enjoyed immense success for several decades.

The Saatchi brothers' magic touch is a continuation of the characteristic streak of success that runs through the commercial résumés of Anglo-Iraqi entrepreneurs of Baghdadi-Jewish descent. Nineteenth-century banker and philanthropist Sir Albert Abdullah David Sassoon, 1st Baronet KCB CSI, was known as the 'Indian Rothschild', since he was a major benefactor to Bombay – the first city he migrated to from Baghdad. Sassoon died in Brighton in 1896 and has rested in Willesden's Jewish cemetery since 1933.

The late Manchester-born property magnate Jack Dellal was also of Baghdadi-Jewish descent. Alan Yentob, creative director of the BBC, also shares Dellal's Iraqi-Jewish lineage, as well as a Manchester childhood.

Judaism has been the main faith in Israel and the Palestinian areas since the formation of the State of Israel in 1948. Palestinian migration to the UK was a result of Israeli settlement on their ancestral lands. Small numbers of Palestinians naturally made their way to Britain – the country had ruled Palestine during this period and their main foreign language was English. As is the case for most colonised nations, the home country of the coloniser is a draw to the oppressed.

South London-born Shadia Mansour is of Palestinian heritage and has been crowned First Lady of Arab hip-hop due to her opposition of Israel's occupation of Palestine via the microphone of urban music – a far cry from the musical genres of her homeland. 'It's about showing support and that there are Palestinians in the diaspora who want to promote their identity and culture,' she says.

It is a surprise that Britain is not home to more Palestinians. Not every Englishman is aware that the Arab League, or League of Arab States, was originally proposed by Great Britain in 1942, as part of a strategy to mobilise Arab countries against the Axis powers during the Second World War. The league was founded in Egypt in 1945 and originally comprised six nations: Egypt, Iraq, Jordan (then Transjordan), the Lebanon, Saudi Arabia and Syria. The Arab League now has twenty-two independent member states within north and north-east Africa and south-west Asia. Many citizens of Arab League nations have migrated to Britain since the end of the Second World War and have formed distinct cultural communities, bonded with a shared common language and religion – mainly Arabic and predominantly Islam and Judaism.

British Israelis appear to have a much larger population than British Palestinians. The majority of them follow the Jewish faith and have long lived in London particularly, but also elsewhere. Many Israeli migrants even complain that they are excluded from the deep-rooted British Jewish community, despite living in mainly Jewish areas. Others remain indifferent to their 'frosty' reception and do not wish to be absorbed by long-standing local Jewish communities.

British comedian and actor Sacha Baron Cohen, whose mother is Israeli, has made an exceptional living trading nationality stereotypes both on the UK small screen and in Hollywood movies. Spoon-bending entertainer Uri Geller and former Chelsea manager Avram Grant are both Israeli migrants to the UK too.

*   *   *

Religion differentiates Middle Eastern migrants as much as ethnicity. Although Islam is the region's dominant religion, it is a diverse faith comprised of variant sects. The majority of Middle Eastern Muslims belong to the Sunni sect of Islam. Egypt, Jordan and Saudi Arabia have the largest Sunni populations, at 90 per cent or more. The Shiite or Shia sect makes up the remaining 10 per cent and are the majority in Bahrain, Iran and Iraq. Smaller Islamic sects include the Alawites, the Druze, the Ibadis, the Shafis and a number of Sufi orders.

The Ismaili sect is led by British citizen the Aga Khan, whose mother – Princess Tajuddawlah Aly Khan – was born Joan Barbara Yarde-Buller. The mother of his heir, Prince Rahim Aga Khan, is the Princess Salimah Aga Khan, formerly English fashion model Sarah Frances Croker-Poole. By his ethnic majority, it could be said that an Englishman will soon be the next spiritual leader of the world's twelve million Ismaili Muslims. Positive proof of the multiculturalism fostered on British soil, and a first-class example of generational integration and genetic assimilation. The Ismaili ease at multicultural integration saw the harmoniously designed Ismaili centre fit seamlessly into the period architecture of Kensington's Cromwell Road. The Ismaili community – which has been present in the UK since the establishment of a centre for Ismaili religion, culture and socialising in 1951 – should have an even stronger cultural presence in 2051.

A 100,000 square-foot Islamic cultural centre and university of similar size, backed by the Aga Khan Development Network, is planned for development within the regenerated King's Cross.

Britain is now home to one of the world's most notable

migrant Muslim populations. British-Muslims form the nation's second-largest religious group. The 2011 Census recorded that 4.8 per cent of the British population (2.7 million people) are Muslim.

As noted within the south Asian and African experiences, this prominent demographic has prompted national debate on how areas of Islam impact upon wider British life and culture, including: the introduction of segregation in state schools; the practice of halal slaughter; the debate on FGM; and the sexual exploitation of white English girls by Muslim men in some marginalised social communities.

Indeed, as well as providing Britain with specialist skills and financial inflows, Muslim migration has also brought a wave of dissidents, radical outlaws and resistance figures. Extreme Islamist groups banned in their own countries have cast a dangerous shadow over Britain's multicultural society. Radical clerics have indoctrinated the socially vulnerable at leading mosques, converting the disaffected to menaces to society and mass killers. The 7/7 bombers took inspiration from al-Qaeda, while Christian-born Michael Adebolajo, the British-Nigerian killer of Fusilier Lee Rigby, was radicalised to commit *jihad* within the UK. He absorbed the hateful preaching of the hook-handed Imam Abu Hamza, who once led the Finsbury Park mosque in north London. In spring 2014, the Egyptian rabble-rouser – who survived on state benefits and a diet of anti-western bile – was convicted on American terrorism charges.

Many would be surprised to learn that Britain's first Islamic place of worship, the Liverpool Muslim Institute, was founded in 1887 by Liverpudlian convert Abdullah Quilliam – born into a wealthy Manx family as William Henry Quilliam – and a Mrs Elizabeth Cates.

Cates and Quilliam's weekly and monthly publications *The Crescent* and the *Islamic World* attracted an international readership spanning twenty countries – proof positive that segments of the British public were more accepting and embracing of Middle Eastern migrants and their way of life in the 1890s than some are in the 2010s. Incidentally, 2 Glynrhondda Street in Cardiff was once erroneously accepted as the United Kingdom's first mosque – it was said to have been in use in 1860 by Somali and Yemeni sailors. The site remains a cornerstone of the Welsh Muslim community, though, under the name of the Al-Manar Islamic & Cultural Centre.

The long-standing presence of Muslim migrants in the UK has made it easier for new groups to find their feet in a foreign land – this has given a measure of solace to refugees fleeing war, especially. Significant refugee migration to Britain has been from Iraq. In the 1960s, Communist Party officials arrived after the Baathist takeover of government. As the home of Iraqi opposition, a further wave of refugees from the Iran–Iraq War of the 1980s found an ease of integration too. The Gulf War refugees who arrived during and after 1991 contributed to the heterogeneity of the UK's Iraqi population, mainly comprised of Arabs, Assyrians and Kurds.

However, Iraqi migrants should not be viewed as solely

refugees from war dependent on social housing. Dame Zaha Hadid was born into an upper-class Sunni Muslim Arab family in 1950s Baghdad. From her Bauhaus home in the Iraqi capital, she grew into a woman who would blaze an architectural trail around the globe. In a double-whammy of success, Hadid was the first woman and first Muslim to win the Pritzker Architecture Prize in 2004. She was awarded the Royal Institute of British Architects' Stirling Prize in 2010 and again in 2011. The heavy workload and hallowed status of a titan of the architectural world has additional dimensions for a woman of Iraqi descent. Hadid has no regrets about not building the family she may have enjoyed had she not left Iraq, but she does admit that: 'If I'd stayed in the Middle East, I could have done it. The family relationships there make it easier to look after children.'

The Iranian equation

Britain's Middle Eastern community is not wholly Arab. Indeed, as the Persian proverb expounds: 'It is better to flee and stay alive than to die and become a hero.' Iran, whose citizens are of Persian ethnicity, with a 2 per cent minority ethnic Arab population, have made a powerful impact on British industry and society. One of the most iconic faces of British fashion is half Iranian – Yasmin Le Bon was born Yasmin Parvaneh to an English mother and an Iranian father in Oxford.

Model dynasty: Yasmin Le Bon has handed the fashion mantle down to the next generation. Her daughter Amber has followed in her fabulous footsteps to become a successful British model.

Brains as well as beauty are the property of many British Iranians. They achieve high economic success. The BBC Born Abroad study found 24.19 per cent of settled Iranians were found to be employed in highly paid jobs. Accomplished business acumen should come as no surprise. The majority of Britain's Iranian community arrived after the 1979 revolution, which resulted in the establishment of the Islamic Republic of Iran. Many migrants came from upper-class and merchant backgrounds. Within five years, around 8,000 Iranians sought asylum in the UK. The 1981 Census recorded 28,617 people born in Iran; the 2011 Census showed that 82,000 Iranian-born residents arrived in the 1970s.

Britain's Iranian community is religiously diverse, which may have played a key role in migration. Iran is primarily Shia, with Bahá'í, Christian, Jewish and Zoroastrian communities. Some Iranians in the UK have converted to Christianity, and the number of Iranian agnostics and atheists has risen. The second generation is quite young as fewer adults of Iranian descent were born and raised in Britain. During the late 1980s and early '90s, Iranian cultural identity grew in the UK with the introduction of Persian media, libraries and language schools, as well as increased religious and business activity.

Notable Iranian-born Britons who have changed the face of British society include Camila Batmanghelidjh CBE, founder of two indispensable charities – the place2b and Kids Company. She and her team care for 17,000 marginalised and vulnerable children and young people in London, and work with forty-one inner-city schools. Batmanghelidjh was born into a privileged Tehran family who supported the Shah of Iran. The 1979 revolution had as huge an impact on their lives as hers had on the futures of many marginalised British youths.

The Tchenguiz siblings take the town

Robert and Vincent Tchenguiz, the property tycoon brothers whose stratospheric success was brought low after an unlawful arrest by the Serious Fraud Office, were born in Tehran. Their father was an Iraqi-Jewish jeweller who settled in Iran in 1948 to work for the Shah and run the Iranian mint. Vincent Tchenguiz's stratospheric commercial success was built upon a solid international academic foundation, which is the hallmark of many Iranian professionals. He completed his studies in Iran in 1973, and then began a business administration course at Boston University, which was followed by two BScs at McGill University in Montreal, and an MA in business administration from New York University. He honed his money-making skills as a trader in the City of London before founding the commercial property business Rotch Property Group with his brother. Funded by cheap debt, Rotch grew to become one of Britain's biggest landlords, owning 250,000 residential freeholds and landmark commercial buildings. The brothers went on to pursue divergent successful paths, but both faltered spectacularly due to a Serious Fraud Office investigation in 2011.

Many who have accrued the capital necessary to take a leap into more creative and risky enterprises now do so with confidence and gusto. In spring 2014, former City worker Vida Tayebi moved into the canteen and launched her fresh enterprise Dindin Kitchen on London's Gray's Inn Road.

Indeed, Iranians have begun to carve their cultural mark

upon the UK via the primary handle of cuisine. Jamshid Golshan Ebrahimi and his acclaimed cookbook-writing English wife Sally Butcher are exceptional ambassadors for Iranian culture and cuisine, with their authentic Middle Eastern delicatessen and café Persepolis transporting a multi-sensual slice of Persia to the heart of Peckham in south-east London – home to many vibrant and ethnically diverse migrant communities.

* * *

Asma al-Assad, the Syrian First Lady, is, by birthright, free to enter the UK if she so chooses, but political migrants from the Arab Spring nations do not have such easy theoretical access. Britain has refused to join the UN resettlement programme and has admitted a mere 500 refugees from Syria. Syrians legally within the UK are able to apply to extend their visas, but they have no access to public funds. Home Office concessions to Syrian citizens within the UK are in force until February 2015.

Thousands of north African migrants have fled Tunisia and Libya since the Arab Spring revolutions and have entered Italy by sea since. Once upon Italian soil, unobstructed travel throughout the European Union is possible. Some political migrants from the Arab Spring have died after overcrowded vessels have sunk en route to Europe. Many migrants who have managed to survive the treacherous waters have used their wits to travel across several countries, risk death and avoid imprisonment in order to achieve their end goal of entering the UK.

In the summer of 2014, the British press reported extensively on the 'jungle' camps of Calais, France, and the violent clashes between Eritrean and Sudanese migrants. Makeshift migrant camps, one known as Jungle 2, have been illegally erected within Calais's forests to house both migrants from the Arab Spring conflicts and east Africans intent on entering the UK – which is easier to do since the reopening of Libya's ports. Libya had long stated that it would help migrants reach Europe if the EU was not forthcoming in granting financial aid to deal with the influx of migrants. Between January and April 2014, the EU border agency Frontex recorded 25,650 migrants entering from Libya.

Phillipe Mignonent, chief of Calais's immigration, spoke of the 'serious pressure' Calais was under as migrants sought to start new lives in the UK; he predicted the camps could be holding over 5,000 migrants by the end of 2014. He also estimated that over thirty migrants make their way across the Channel each day. Mignonent supports Calais's mayor Natacha Bouchart's building of a facility similar to the Red Cross Sangatte camp, which housed 2,000 migrants prior to its closure in 2002, and ignited a crisis in UK immigration. 'What we want to do is buy the migrants ferry tickets to Britain and let them deal with the problem … We want the border to be moved from Calais to Dover and Folkestone for one month so Britain understands how difficult the problem is.'

If Mr Mignonent follows through with this threat, Britain will experience a boom in Arabic-speaking summer visitors with less spending money than those it is currently accustomed to hosting.

Spending the summer in the capital city

'They absolutely don't want summer sales bargains; they want new season stock. They're very keen on fine jewellery and shoes, and on recognised brands like Chanel. They're very savvy shoppers and they want the latest, most fashionable, limited-edition products,' a Selfridges spokesperson noted of the affluent Middle Eastern shoppers who, in the summer of 2012, shopped as if the practice were a seasonal sport.

Lebanese businessman Said Chaarawi's consultancy – Understanding Arabia – enables the capital's luxury boutiques and department stores to provide customer service bespoke to Arab culture during the seasonal shopping boom known as the 'Ramadan Rush' – which provides London businesses with substantial annual profits . For example, a male sales associate will hand a jewel-encrusted necklace or solid gold watch to a female customer's husband – for him to assist his wife's perusal – rather than attempt to secure it around her neck or wrist himself. Such a cultural faux pas could jeopardise sales and jobs, which the retail sector and economy at large depend upon.

This gold-plated consumption meant that Arab tourism boosted London sales by 36 per cent, upped employment by 13.5 per cent, and contributed to the revival of the city's hospitality sector. In 2012, Saudi tourists spent £78 million on London hotel bookings – tips to chambermaids and chauffeurs were not counted. But HM Revenue and Customs gains more than even the most appreciated five-star butler could ever dream of in 'tips', as most Gulf Coast tourists leave the country without claiming a single VAT refund.

The new eastern order

Makhtoum, Al-Thani, Saud...

Some Arabian surnames are just as well known to readers of the pink pages of the *FT* as they are to those who scour the glossy pages of *Hello!* magazine. Not since the oil boom of the 1970s has Britain witnessed such an outpouring of financial capital invested in UK trade and industry by Arab economic migrants.

Egyptian business magnate Mohamed Al-Fayed – who was twice unsuccessful in gaining British citizenship – owned and successfully developed the quintessentially British retail institution Harrods. Since 2010, the Knightsbridge department store has belonged to the Qatari royal family's investment company Qatari Holding. Al-Fayed's pharaonic totems remain in situ and, despite not gaining British citizenship, he is the owner of 65,000 acres of Scotland.

* * *

Moving into luxury retail in one of Europe's most fashionable and creative cities was a masterstroke of commercial and cultural strategy in both the short and long term for Qatar. The emirate's £50 billion sovereign wealth fund is led by Sheikh Hamad bin

Khalifa Al Thani, aka 'London's Landlord'. The Olympic Village and Chelsea Barracks were also acquired by him and funding was given to the Shard and One Hyde Park. Indeed, the most valuable apartment in the latter building – the world's most expensive apartment block – is said to be owned by the Sheikh … his version of living above the corner shop, as was the norm for earlier migrants.

Record-breaking art buyer: Sheikha al Mayassa runs the Qatar Museums Authority and spends big without ever breaking the bank.

The next generation of Qatari business moguls find it easier to follow in their fathers' gilded footsteps. Sheikha al Mayassa – daughter to Sheikh Hamad and the influential Sheikha Mozah, as well as sister to Qatar's new Emir – contributes greatly to London's economy. Her $1 billion art acquisition budget has a great trickle-down effect on the capital, and her artistic patronage makes it rain revenue on London institutions such as the V&A,

which successfully hosted the Pearls exhibition in conjunction with the Qatar Museums Authority between September 2013 and January 2014. Mayassa is also reputed to have sponsored Damien Hirst's major Tate retrospective of 2012. The artists, galleries and museums in the rest of England hope that the tidal wave of artistic funding hits them some time soon.

The UK's Arab residents tend to stick to London, in a style to which they have long been accustomed. Visitors from Saudi Arabia and the Gulf – some staying for a three-month holiday – demand and enjoy the best that London has to offer. They provide the capital's retailers, niche businesses (including close-protection bodyguard companies and concierge services such as Quintessentially) and hospitality providers – as well as the British government, via taxation – with a seasonal windfall each year.

Stateswoman in the making: Amal Clooney adds a 21st-century Middle Eastern twist to women 'having it all'.

London may yet experience greater social and economic windfalls since the marriage of Hollywood actor and political aspirant George Clooney to the multi-faceted international law and human rights barrister Amal Alamuddin in October 2014. The high-profile match shone a light on a little-known British minority group – the Druze sect of the Lebanon. The Druze practise a unique religion, established in Egypt and north Africa in the eleventh century, that carries the core principles of Islam – although the Druze are not considered Muslims. Incidentally, during a war in 1860 between the Lebanon's Druze and Christians, the Druze were supported by the British.

Mrs Clooney – whose British post-wedding bash was held at Danesfield House Hotel, an English Heritage house now owned by fellow Druze Lebanese businessman Salim Khaireddine – is a remarkable example of what second-generation migrants often make of themselves with great generational role models. Clooney's maiden name Alamuddin points to her paternal descent from the sheikhs of Lebanon's Baaqline municipality. Her mother, Baaria Meknas, carved a prominent niche for herself as a journalist and political commentator at the pan-Arab media house Al-Hayat.

Clooney was born in Beirut and raised in Buckinghamshire. She attended a grammar school and won a scholarship to Oxford's St Hugh's College before gaining a master of laws at New York University Law School. Like many gifted migrant children afforded the opportunities and advantages of an exceptional education, Clooney has granted others insight into her birth culture, and has offered expertise to many Middle Eastern nations since being called to the Bar in 2010. She has trained police forces in the Gulf, acted as a senior legal advisor to the prosecutor of the Special Tribunal for Lebanon, advised Special Envoy Kofi Annan on Syria, and counsels the royal court of Bahrain on reforms to ensure international human rights compliance. In her role as a criminal barrister, she has represented Libya's former intelligence chief, Abdallah Al Senussi, against allegations of crimes against humanity at the International Criminal Court, and she was also a member of the prosecution against four defendants accused of assassinating the former Lebanese Prime Minister Hariri at the Special Tribunal for Lebanon in the Hague. She served as rapporteur for the International Bar Association Human Rights Institute, focusing on the independence of Egypt's judiciary after the 2011 revolution. Clooney seems tipped for even greater success, but in which country might this be? Will she become the first woman of UK background to rise to the position of First Lady of the United States of America since London-born Louisa Johnson Adams gained the title in 1825?

* * *

Some of Britain's Middle Eastern migrants have proven adept at rising high in British society and enhancing the nation's quality of life. In November 2014, the General Medical Council recorded that 2,370 UK practising doctors gained their Primary

Medical Qualification in Iraq. It is a testament to the success of our multicultural society that, even during times of war – previously Iraq, and currently Syria – when a disaffected minority risk losing their British citizenship to wage *jihad* in the Middle East, other well-qualified Middle Eastern migrants from war-ravaged and politically unstable nations have sought and received refuge in Britain. The Hippocratic Oath transcends national boundaries and political realities. These immigrants pledge to resuscitate British lives as valuable registered medical practitioners and they continue to preserve and save these lives in hospitals and clinics near you. The infusion of value-adding migrants, who ensure that the UK is a robust nation fit enough to tackle and survive hostilities both physically and economically, embodies the true 'Blitz spirit' – a lesson to us all in terms of national resilience and rejuvenation.

Chapter 8

The eastern European and Polish communities

THE YEAR 2004 DOES SEEM to have been a major water-shed in UK immigration. This was the year Tony Blair's Labour government granted full rights to citizens of the new accession EU member states to live and work in Britain. Not to just anyone, mind you – just to Poland. Also to the Czechs, the Estonians and the Latvians. That's it, no one else. Unless you count the Slovenians, Lithuanians and Slovaks. And the Hungarians, obviously. We definitely need them too.

Clearly, in retrospect, the plan was that the politicians would pretend they were all Romanians – who were not at all part of this so-called 'A8' – and put all the blame on them when it went wrong. But that's alright. The only other EU member states that adopted an equally relaxed approach to immigration from the A8 countries were Ireland and Sweden, so what could have gone wrong with that idea? A brilliant plan.

The Blair government thought some eastern Europeans may be tempted to live and work in Britain, but wholly underestimated the numbers. Nor did the Labour government fully appreciate the potential demand for their skills from employers frustrated by the struggle to recruit motivated local workers who could be relied upon to turn up on time. After all, as the American writer and film director Woody Allen points out, showing up is 80 per cent of life. Far too often, employers found that, when they hired local British employees, they did not even show up for work – this was particularly true for farmers and market gardening businesses in counties like Lincolnshire and Kent.

As of 2004, Poles and other citizens from A8 countries were given full rights to settle and work in Britain – so long as they observed the Worker Registration Scheme. They had certain limitations placed on their access to benefits under the UK welfare state, but otherwise they were treated like UK citizens. Significantly, our eastern European guests made little use of the British welfare state, preferring instead to work and look after each other – often through the Roman Catholic Church, which saw a boom in attendance thereby triggering a new demand for Polish-speaking priests.

The official figures set out the extent of what has proved to be the largest short-term peacetime shift in population across Europe in modern history. Gross immigration from the A8 to the UK after accession in 2004 spiralled to 711,000 over the eight-year period of 2004 to 2012. Annual net immigration was never less than 60,000 and, in the year ending June 2013, it totalled 106,000. The 2011 Census indicates that no fewer than 2.7 million residents of England and Wales were born in other EU countries. Furthermore, around 41 per cent of them – 1.1 million – were born in countries which joined the EU in 2004 or later.

One has to remember that many of those who moved to Britain looking for work have come and gone: since 2002 almost 1.2 million Poles have been issued with National Insurance numbers, however many of them returned to Poland as the zloty strengthened against the pound and the Polish economy gained momentum.

People are surprised to discover that Poles have, nonetheless, now become the second-largest foreign-born group after Indians. According to the 2011 Census, 579,000 of them now reside in Britain, a ten-fold increase from a decade earlier, and around 27 per cent of all Polish-born residents in England and Wales live in London. But that means that over 70 per cent live in the regions. In 2012, Polish women gave birth to 21,156 children, more than any other group apart from women who were born in Britain.

What is striking about this wave of eastern European

immigration is the way in which they have ventured across the length and breadth of the British Isles. Even in the Highlands of Scotland you are likely to meet an immigrant from eastern Europe, often working in one of the local hotels or bars. They even work as guides at those most iconic of establishments – Scotch whisky distilleries. Fortunately, the Americans think their accent is Scottish.

For the east Europeans to be that welcomed and have penetrated that ubiquitously, there has to be a real need. Whitehall predictions reckoned that annual immigration from A8 countries would merely amount to 13,000 – an unrealistically low figure. Labour's former Home Secretary, Jack Straw, calls the decision by his party to grant citizens of EU accession states free access to Britain a 'spectacular mistake'. But it cannot seriously be claimed there was no need, if such numbers so easily found jobs everywhere they went.

A compelling case can be made to say that Britain has benefitted greatly from this wave of immigration. Over the last decade or more, service standards and productivity have been transformed across a broad spectrum of industries because of the contribution made by eastern European workers, none more so than the construction sector, along with hotels and hospitality, horticulture and agriculture, and the care industry.

As *The Economist* points out, 'Britain got younger and better-educated Poles than Germany or America. Many are overqualified for their jobs, and ought to move into more appropriate ones as their English and social networks become stronger.'

Too busy for crime then. Researchers at the LSE and University College London say that recorded crime and anti-social behaviour in Corby, a town that attracted many A8 immigrants, has fallen by more than half since 2006; in the rest of England and Wales it is down by about a third.

However, immigration from EU accession countries has put inevitable pressure on Britain's social infrastructure, especially in some small rural towns such as Boston, Lincolnshire. Over the four-year period from 2008 to 2012, the number of Polish pupils in England doubled to 54,000. This has increased competition for school places, particularly at good schools. Terrible, you say? No wonder the school results have suffered? I don't think so.

In Peterborough, a town with a sizeable influx of Polish immigrants, the share of pupils getting five good GCSEs rose from 37.2 per cent in 2008 to 57.7 per cent this year, just below the national average of 60.2 per cent. Furthermore, many Polish kids go to school on Saturday as well, in order to maintain their language and culture. These Polish kids are in a hurry to get on in the world.

So, Tony Blair deserves a more favourable legacy. He gave the nation the immense benefit of a second electable political party, a minimum wage, academy schools, a slightly saner House of Lords, and, most importantly, the Polish builder. His historical star will rise again (Iraq being, thankfully, outside the scope of this book) and, if there is any justice, it will be a Polish mason who carves on Tony's tombstone: 'Thanks for the hand-up of history.'

*   *   *

It wasn't all down to Tony, though. In the case of the Baltic states, one can trace a long tradition of people settling in Britain. Over a century ago, many Latvian and Lithuanian refugees began to settle in and around Glasgow. Sir Matt Busby's forebears were among them. Some of these refugees were Jewish families seeking to escape persecution. Many came to Scotland as they could not afford the journey on to America; others were even duped into thinking they had arrived in America, only to subsequently discover they were, in fact, in Scotland.

By the 1950s, there were over 10,000 immigrants from the Baltic states living in and around Glasgow, their numbers reinforced by exiles from the communist annexation of the Baltic countries. But this figure palls when compared with the 2011 UK Census, which found that 97,083 Lithuanians were residing in the UK – a large rise from a population of fewer than 5,000 in 2001. The number of expatriate workers from Latvia has meanwhile climbed from about 7,000 in 2004, to an estimated 39,000 in 2011.

Immigration from other Warsaw Pact countries has not been as great as that from Poland. However, in terms of immigration as a proportion of the total national population, Slovakia ranks as the fastest-growing foreign-born group living and working in the UK, albeit from a relatively modest base. There are now over 52,000 of them resident in Britain. This represents a six-fold jump since 2004, when there were only an estimated 8,000 Slovaks living in the UK.

Czech immigration is characterised by tragedy and courage. The Jewish population bore the brunt of Nazi terror tactics, and yet, alert to this menace, Sir Nicholas George Winton (a remarkable gentleman born in Hampstead, north London, to German parents) rescued no fewer than 669 children – many of whom were Jewish – by personally organising their escape from Czechoslovakia on the eve of the Second World War. This episode has gone down in history as the Czech Kindertransport: a train was reserved to convey the children to a Dutch port and then on to England. The train was actually locked so no one could alight on the journey as it trundled through the continent. There is a statue to these lucky children at Liverpool Street station, where many of them were greeted by British families who had volunteered to offer them a home. Many of these children grew up to make an outstanding contribution to British life. Among them were Alf Dubs – the Labour MP for Battersea (now Lord Dubs) – and Paul Ritter – the distinguished architect and planner. Sir Nicholas Winton set a truly remarkable example of personal commitment and courage. In October 2014, at the admirable age of 105, he was awarded the Order of the White Lion by Czech President Milos Zeman during a ceremony at Prague Castle. It is the highest honour offered by the government of the Czech Republic.

The Kindertransport memorial at Liverpool Street station, London: a new life in Britain beckons.

Other notable refugees from the Czech Republic include Karel Reisz – who was responsible for a string of memorable movies including *Saturday Night and Sunday Morning, This Sporting Life* and *The French Lieutenant's Woman* – and Sir Tom Stoppard – the award-winning playwright and co-author of the screenplay for *Shakespeare in Love*, who went on to receive perhaps the most distinguished award bestowed by the Queen, namely the Order of Merit. Sadly, while Sir Tom managed to escape the Czech Republic via Singapore in 1939, when he was only a child, his father was less fortunate and died in Japanese captivity. Much of Sir Tom Stoppard's dramatic work has focused on human rights, censorship and political freedom. In Britain he found the freedom to speak out – one among many. We should be proud of what Britain represents in the world in this regard.

* * *

Official estimates suggest that as many as 40,000 Czech-born immigrants are currently living in Britain. This is noticeably lower than the contingent from Poland, but similar to the numbers from Hungary. Immigration from Hungary actually took quite a while to accelerate after the Blair reforms, though. In the late 1950s, some Hungarians had fled to Britain as political asylum seekers following the bloody suppression by the Russians of the 1956 uprising against the communist government. However, this was not a significant inflow and the British government did not make it particularly easy for them to enter the country.

Polling evidence indicates that, in this current decade, Hungarians, particularly the younger, well-educated ones, are eager to find employment abroad. Research surveys by Ipsos indicate that one-third of the young generation is planning to find employment abroad. It turns out their destination of choice is Britain, specifically London, which is perceived as 'cool' and a vibrant city that offers a myriad range of employment opportunities. The Hungarian Facebook group *Londonfalva* ('London Village'), which plays a vital role in organising

London's Hungarian community, therefore boasts over 22,000 members.

The 2011 British Census listed 44,000 individuals in England and Wales who said that Hungarian was their mother tongue. Over the past ten years, the NHS has registered almost 100,000 Hungarians, albeit these statistics omit children and those adults who are self-employed or in unregistered jobs.

Among the Hungarians to settle in Britain in the post-war era was George Mikes, the author of *How to be an Alien* – a primer that deals with crucial English topics such as the weather, the love of queuing, taking tea and how not to be too clever (which Mikes notices is regarded by many locals as bad manners). On the sensitive subject of the British and their private life, Mike penned a commendably short chapter, which simply observed that: 'Continental people have sex lives; the English have hot water bottles.'

* * *

Croatia was only admitted into the EU in 2013. In contrast to the experience with A8 countries, the UK has ruled that citizens of Croatia will have to wait seven years before they can take up jobs in Britain. Croatia's national unemployment rate is over 20 per cent and, among its young people, that figure climbs to more than 50 per cent. These high rates clearly concern the British authorities – and coalition government ministers – who were understandably reluctant to see a further wave of eastern European immigrants heading for our shores. Consequently, the drawbridge was raised, although some determined immigrants still manage to make a life for themselves here.

Bulgaria and Romania have recently attracted considerable media attention, centring on whether they represent a new tsunami of EU immigration. A report from the OECD published in 2013 highlighted the fact that citizens from the 'Club Med' countries – Greece, Spain and Italy – have been flocking to Britain and Germany in search of work because there is none to be found back home. The OECD estimates that the numbers looking for work in Britain have doubled since the financial recession of 2007/8. In 2011, Britain saw 88,000 people arrive from southern European countries eager to find work, while Germany received 78,000. This is mainly based on the quantity of National Insurance numbers issued to overseas nationals in Britain.

In the case of Bulgaria and Romania, the UK government laid down tighter restrictions on their ability to find work here in Britain. It was only in January 2014 that the final curbs were relaxed. In light of the shambles over forecasting immigration from Poland and the Baltic states, the coalition government sensibly refrained from making any predictions relating to immigration flows. Clearly, Whitehall had learned some painful lessons from the Blair years. But this did not stop MPs such as Keith Vaz – always keen to spot a photo opportunity – rushing to Luton airport to greet Romanian workers off a no-frills airline. He was disappointed with what he saw: there was hardly a stampede of new arrivals and the signs suggest that most Romanians and Bulgarians who wanted to move here had already done so under the guise of being self-employed workers. Furthermore, over 10,000 Romanians and Bulgarians already study in UK universities.

In practice, both Romanians and Bulgarians have been able to move to the UK for work since 2007. According to the official statistics, 118,000 of them moved to Britain in a five-year period. It turns out that many Romanians prefer to move to Italy, since its language, culture and weather are more familiar. In contrast to 2004, when the A8 joined the EU, several other major economies within the union – notably France, Germany and Italy – have also relaxed controls on immigration from the so-called A2 accession member states. In 2004, though, they kept the barriers to immigration firmly in place.

Research into Romanian and Bulgarian immigration in this country since 2006 – by the left-of-centre think tank, the IPPR – reveals that most of these new arrivals are younger and healthier than the population as a whole. They are also more likely to be in work and paying taxes, which means that they are less likely to be drawing state benefits. What is more, a high proportion of them are concentrated in high-skill jobs and professions. Britain has also greatly profited from recruiting a substantial number of seasonal agricultural work over the past seven years. The Migration Advisory

Committee (MAC), in its report on the Seasonal Agricultural Workers Scheme, points out that up to 21,250 A2 citizens a year have been officially employed under this scheme since 2008; there were probably a lot more unrecorded hires, too. Many of them are highly qualified students and graduates: they even tend to speak more grammatically correct English than the locals. The MAC observed that the scheme was a success both for growers, who were able to draw on an efficient workforce (with knock-on benefits for supermarkets and consumers), and for the people working on the scheme itself, who were paid well. The committee concluded that the scheme had not displaced British workers – but that was probably because the locals were not actually interested in doing this type of work.

It is impressive to discover the substantial number of entrepreneurs who have come from A2 and other eastern European countries to start businesses in the UK. Why is this the case? Well, they have spotted London's leading position as a global hub for financial services, as well as its pre-eminent position in many creative industries such as fashion, film-editing and music.

* * *

While Britain has clearly benefitted in many ways from the wave of eastern European immigration witnessed over the last decade, it is also true that considerable concerns and tensions have been generated by the prospect and experience of Roma gypsies moving to Britain. For many years, Roma travellers have sought political asylum in this country, but, in general, they have been turned down. For instance, in the two years leading up to the accession of the A8 countries in 2004, there were almost 100 per cent refusal rates for all Roma citizens applying for asylum from the Czech Republic, Poland and Romania.

Across Europe, Roma travellers are associated with aggressive begging, rough sleeping and criminality of various sorts. This may or may not be true, but the perception is ubiquitous.

Although there is undoubtedly a criminal element, discrimination and poor living standards are key drivers of migration among Roma people. Romania and Bulgaria are no different from other eastern European countries in giving short shrift to their Roma communities. The statistics reflect the fact that they struggle to find jobs and their educational attainment is below the national average.

Overall, it is perhaps the east Europeans who have become the most favoured topical whipping boys for the political classes. And yet, I recall that many of the MPs, who now regularly express concern over east European immigration, somehow first managed to have their London flats superbly renovated by Poles at rather a good price. For some miraculous reason, their essential new plaster is always set and their second-home paint always dry before they come to realise just how 'concerned' they really are.

Case study: Remus Azoitei

Hitting a high note in his new home

The Royal Academy of Music appointed Remus Azoitei as a violin professor in 2002. At the time, he was the youngest person to attain this illustrious title in the institution's history. Remus was born in 1971 in Galati, a town in eastern Romania, during the communist era. His prodigious musical talent was identified at an early age and nurtured by his parents despite the myriad restrictions of the Ceauşescu regime.

'You couldn't move between cities. You were designated a town to live in and you couldn't just leave that city and go to Bucharest or another town. My parents had to move mountains for this.' Remus was lucky enough to be granted permission to resettle and study away from his home town. He moved to Bucharest at twelve years old and progressed to playing the violin, graduating from all of the Bucharest conservatoire schools. Between 1995 and 1998, Remus taught violin at the Bucharest Conservatoire, enriching the musical development of the younger guard of Romanian violinists.

Talent and hard work reap dividends and pave the way for exceptional opportunities. For those living in restrictive societies or within dictatorial regimes, an investment in exceptional skills in areas such as the arts, sport and science can allow them to transcend their social circumstance and build a glittering future beyond their home borders.

At the age of twenty-five, Remus won a scholarship to the Juilliard School in New York, considered the highest musical education institution in the world. He spent three years completing the master's course and was tutored by titans of the classical music world, including Dorothy DeLay, Masao Kawasaki, and the legendary Israeli-American violinist Itzhak Perlman.

> It was a great experience – a different world all together. I enjoyed living in New York though it never clicked with me deep down – people are always in a rush and I found them rather superficial. However, in terms of education excellence, unsurpassable. I always return to NY for concerts and I think fondly of my time there.

Remus's palpable talent attracted attention from across the Atlantic. After graduating from Juilliard in 2001, he was offered a professorship of violin. 'The Royal Academy of Music is a very conservative institution and, being thirty-one, I was the youngest ever professor in the 200-year history.' His students have proven very successful and, as a result, he is in high demand.

> I am extremely, extremely honoured and pleased to offer my musical services to a society like Britain and, of course, I am a product of multicultural zones and knowledge. The way I teach the violin and make music, of course, is highly polished in the western side of the world, but it will always

bear the Romanian soul, which is at the seed of everything
I do, and my English students benefit from this enormously.

In 2004, Remus won the title of Associate of the Royal Academy of Music due to his professional achievements. He also
completed his PhD in Enescu violin music. The Romanian
composer George Enescu was a great force in twentieth-century
music and is regarded as Romania's most important musician.
He mentored the American-born Yehudi Menuhin, who was
made an honorary Knight Commander of the Order of the
British Empire in 1965 while still an American citizen. Menuhin gained British citizenship in 1985 and, with his knighthood
upgraded, was then known as Sir Yehudi Menuhin KBE. In
1987, he was also appointed a member of the Order of Merit by
Queen Elizabeth II. Great violinists who have migrated to Britain have richly embroidered the cultural fabric of our society.

Remus's route to Britain and his ascent to the top of the
academic tree have been relatively smooth – if not straightfor-
ward. This is due to his paragon talent and unique skills. Not
many Romanians had the freedom of movement that Remus
was privy to then – and which they enjoy now:

> Back then Romania was not in the EU. There was always this
> procedure that any employee at the Academy or anywhere
> else within the EU institutions had to prove that nobody else
> within the EU could do the job that an outsider can do. This
> proved to be my case.

The Royal Academy wanted the best man for their professorship post and he happened to be Remus. They applied on his behalf and even handled the intense toing-and-froing of immigration applications, filing supportive cases and ensuring he could join the institution using the framework of employment and immigration laws. The process took around two years. 'It is very difficult in a field as subjective as music to prove that somebody is better than somebody else. Teaching music is such a non-exact business.' Remus ruminated that his application was smooth because 'the Academy was highly supportive and is such a respected institution'. Having a venerable sponsor made for a much more comfortable journey of progress than those encountered by some Romanian migrants, who often entered Britain illegally secreted within haulage trucks. 'Meanwhile, I became an EU citizen with the integration of Romania, but the process had already started and was successful already.'

Back in 2001, Remus had a few Romanian friends in London. The number has increased since 2007, when Romania became part of the EU and freedom of movement attracted many Romanians to the British capital. 'Now there are quite a few of them. Tens of thousands in London, I'd say. Hardworking people, and I believe they bring a lot to the British society.'

Nigel Farage of UKIP dived into hot water with grossly overestimated and xenophobic predictions – which were not realised – of Romanian and Bulgarian hordes flooding British borders when their migration restrictions were lifted on

1 January 2014. A trickle of migrants rather than a deluge were greeted by Home Affairs Select Committee chairman Keith Vaz at Luton airport on the date billed by the media and some politicians as an immigration doomsday. The news dimly flashed that British ports were neither overwhelmed nor relatively busier than usual.

'I don't come to rob your country; I come to work and go home,' thirty-year-old Romanian incomer Victor Spiersau told Vaz over a welcoming cup of English breakfast (or was it builder's) tea, before setting off to begin his waiting car-washing job. The €10 he had earned in a day back home would be paid to him per hour in Britain.

The mission of the migrants, slurred and grossly overestimated in the run-up to 1 January, appears to be to better themselves and increase their standard of living. Spiersau's objective was to earn enough money to renovate his Romanian home and live a better life in his own country. The migrants are coming for economic fulfilment. They have no desire to 'scrounge on the dole' as rhetoric jibes; 'scrounging' is not as easy in practice as sensationalised segments of the gutter press or ignorant idle chatter would suggest. The vast majority are committed to working hard and contributing equally to British society, as well as their dependants and communities back home. The character of the manual class of these new eastern European migrants is reminiscent of the old British working class, who worked hard and saved what they could in an effort to better themselves, build a nest egg and perhaps climb the social ladder in a generation or three. Britons who have fallen to the level of 'underclass' in recent generations would do well to follow the lead of European migrants employed in the positions they do not apply for and deem beneath them. It would certainly reduce the nation's social security bill, and a diet of freshly picked fruit and vegetables bought at staff discount could benefit the NHS via the slashing of certain treatment budgets.

It would certainly be something to see if a burst of economic productivity from fit-to-work but unemployed Britons were to trump the £20 billion contributed to the British economy by EU immigrants between 2001 and 2011.

Is it fair that citizens from the original fifteen EU countries have paid 64 per cent more in tax than they have received in welfare benefits? Is it fair that recent migrants from central and eastern Europe have contributed 12 per cent more to the British economy than they have received in return? Is it fair that we label them all scroungers, when many Britons who are fit to work do anything but?

In this age of globalisation, communication and technology, learning a new language is necessary and not as hard as in past eras. Is the British monolingual habit a throwback from the days of empire or an indication of educational failure? Surely equality within the EU would see more of those graduates who struggle to find work – and those young professionals who find it hard to get a foot on the property ladder – seeking out richer pastures and cheaper mortgages in cities of opportunity such as Frankfurt, Milano and Praha?

Remus, who speaks English with fluency and clarity, is balanced in his appraisal of opportunistic politicians – and political parties – with biased research and myopic insights, who seek to whip up social frenzy and xenophobia in a bid to win votes and an EU referendum:

> I'm also a British citizen so I am able to look from both ends of the tunnel here. My personal opinion is that these people coming here they do pay taxes and do work hard. A lot of Romanians are paying taxes and working hard and doing low-skilled jobs that the English don't want to do and they pay taxes. The only problem I find as a British citizen is that the British government does not recognise or take into account this influx of people into the infrastructure. The British government does not invest to update and expand the roads and the hospitals to accommodate these people who are paying taxes in Britain. These people work, so Britain benefits from them being here. They take all the jobs British people wouldn't like to have. They pay taxes for it, but, in return, they need to be accommodated. So here is the choice: we kick them out or we keep them. But if we keep them we have an obligation to enhance their living and everybody else's. Otherwise what are we doing exactly? We benefit from them but we don't give anything in return.

Remus resents having to spend an hour in London's traffic – due to the huge increase in people – when roads could be developed via the tax mechanisms that accrue revenue from present migrant contributions: 'The people paying taxes here have to be accommodated and integrated. That's where their taxes should go, but I feel this is not the case. The British government does not wake up to the reality of this.'

Freedom of movement was at the core of the creation of the European Union, but it seems to be the core issue on which politicians did not do their homework, figure out their sums, engage their logic, or recall the Commonwealth migration experiences prior to integration with other European nations. Britain has always been attractive to migrants due to our standard of living, way of life and opportunities – and will always remain so. As the saying goes: 'Marry in haste, repent at leisure.'

On the state of the union and current British sentiments, Remus mused: 'My intimate feeling is that the rest of the country feels the pressure of this increase in population. They look at who is coming in rather than what the government should do, since the benefits of their taxes could actually increase the condition of living for everybody.' On the demonisation of the Roma gypsies, who have set up camp amid the prime real estate and elite businesses around Park Lane, Remus explains:

This is almost impossible to contain. The people in the park are not true Romanians; they just have passports written 'Romanian' on it. To be absolutely honest with you, I don't consider anybody being Romanian if they are begging around because Romanians are not about that. They are hard-working people. These are individuals who are hiding behind their Romanian passport – therefore their EU passport – to follow their own interests with total disregard for putting a stain on the people they are coming from.

The Roma gypsies, whose ancient ancestors migrated from northern India to Europe, are motivated to exercise their rights of freedom of movement around Europe by economic factors. 'They come from villages where the poverty is overwhelming. Even begging in Hyde Park is probably better than being in Romania. This is a reality which politicians have to deal with.'

Seeing as we are all in this together as EU member states – country cousins as it were – dealing with such issues is surely a family affair: Britain's problems are Romania's. 'It all comes down to poverty,' states Remus, who has seen the state of the Roma in both of his home countries.

If a country is poor there is no regulation that can be imposed to stop the negative effect of free travel. This is how it is. So, unless both governments, British and Romanian, work together to raise the economic level of Romania or the EU, because we are all in the EU now this will always be a problem.

The standard of living in Romania has risen a great deal since the fall of communism – and continues to do so – but, as in every nation on earth, there will always be disparities of income, wealth and opportunity for social mobility. On the status quo and future of Romania, Remus is insightful: 'My feeling is that they need a bit of help from the EU.' As fellow European citizens in supposed unity, it is noticeable that 'we don't quite assist these developing countries that are struggling a lot. We don't quite look at them as partners. We look at them as liabilities.'

Remus is a fully integrated and enriching migrant who shatters the stereotypes that some would have us believe eastern European migrants represent – gypsies, families leap-frogging council house waiting lists, and builders taking over a traditionally British working-class industry. What does being British mean to him now that he is a citizen? 'I speak English at home, I deal with English people. I work in a very English institution. I play concerts in England. I am anglicised with a Romanian soul. I love this country equally and I am devoted to them both equally.'

Having travelled a great deal in his life and career, Remus adds:

> I can just say one thing: English people are not racist. Really for them, if you are valuable and you are good at what you do, you are a winner and they value you regardless of where you have come from or the colour of your skin – and this, to me, is a sign of a highly developed type of society.

Remus is happily married to an English woman who learned Romanian of her own accord. They have two young children and are very happy in London. They try to visit Romania at least twice each year to see Remus's family. He also teaches masterclasses at the Bucharest Conservatoire, so is balanced in his development of Europe's next generation of violinists. Resettling in Romania has crossed his mind, but the international aspect of his profession makes England a better strategic base. 'Maybe one day when I am very old I will go back there and die happy.'

Professor Christian Dustmann, Director of the UCL Centre for Research and Analysis of Migration (CReAM), noted in November 2014: 'European immigrants particularly, both from the new accession countries and the rest of the European Union, make the most substantial contributions. This is mainly down to their higher average labour market participation compared with natives and their lower receipt of welfare benefits.'

How this great revenue is used remains to be seen.

Chapter 9

The Russian community and post-Soviet republics

RUSSIANS WERE A RARITY IN London in the 1970s, at the height of the Cold War. Yet now they are commonplace and the capital is even referred to as Londongrad. London is only a four-hour flight from Moscow, and schools, restaurants and shopping are good. As I go about London, I hear Russian spoken on the tube, on the bus and in every department store I visit. The Russians love to shop in the nation's capital; they love the city's fundraising power and investment opportunities;

they love being allowed to speak their mind. Freedom is real
– something the Russian establishment still struggles with as
they deploy and protect their despicable overseas assassins.
The polonium murder of Alexander Litvinenko will not be
forgotten. But while the Russian leaders slide back to the cor-
rupted but comforting habits of history, modern Russians love
London and all it represents and offers – and so London loves
them right back.

Britain with its tolerant attitude to foreigners casts many a
lure, particularly to those with money: it is relatively straight-
forward to set up a business; the financial service sector is
extremely well developed and welcoming to Russian money;
and the tax regime for non-doms has proved very enticing to
Russian citizens. What's more, London is generally seen as a
safe place as well as a fashionable city to live in – one of the few
true global cities. For some, there is even a tug from history; it
should be noted that even the Queen strikes a chord in Russia as the Windsors are perceived as cousins of the Romanovs.
Of course, the royal press handlers here are usually not much
keener on that part of the past than they are on the German
ancestry. The nuisance of inconvenient truths.

Britain offers another major attraction to Russians: a functioning independent legal system – something we take for
granted, but should not, and something the Russians cannot
take for granted in their own land. There is a sigh of relief that
comes from simply being surrounded by seriousness about
the rule of law. Our legal system is seen as independent and

transparent. So much so that Russians often bring their disputes with each other to be resolved in the British courts.

Boris Berezovsky: the coroner recorded an open verdict.

The divorce courts are kept busy, but the contractual battle between Roman Abramovich and fellow Russian oligarch Boris Berezovsky was the most high-profile of these cases to date. As the lengthy case unfolded over a twelve-month period, the court heard Mr Berezovsky claim that Mr Abramovich was a 'gangster', while, in response, Mr Abramovich suggested that Mr Berezovsky was 'something of a megalomaniac'. Lawyers are said to have racked up total legal fees of around £100 million by the time the case ended. The verdict went against Mr Berezovsky, who was claiming a total of $6.5 billion in damages with respect to the ownership of Sibneft, an oil company Mr Abromovich subsequently sold to Gazprom. Berezovsky was later found dead in March 2013 at his former wife's country mansion in Ascot. At the inquest held in March 2014, the coroner recorded an open verdict with respect to his death after hearing conflicting expert medical evidence about the circumstances under which Mr Berezovsky's body was found hanged. Professor Bern Brinkmann, an eminent German forensic scientist, submitted a report to the inquest which referred to the possibility that Mr Berezovsky was assassinated by a number of assailants. *Crime and Punishment* Londongrad style?

* * *

Over the last fifteen years, Russia's GDP has expanded ten-fold in dollar terms, from $200 billion to more than $2 trillion – creating, in the process, the world's eighth-largest economy, or sixth-largest, if measured by purchasing power. Arguably, this puts the Russian Federation ahead of both Britain and France.

Truly astonishing then that President Putin would choose to jeopardise this status over the ephemeral gains of its atavistic interference in Ukraine. They won't be celebrating Putin when they reach the end of the cul-de-sac he has led them down – but how many decades will it be before they dare to admit that mistake to themselves. How many billions will now not be invested in the enterprises of the fickle, unpredictable, law-twisting, free-speech-fearing, quixotic darling that is mother

Russia. Well, let Putin drive all the Russian money and potential future investment abroad. A lot of it will finish up in this country, with or without its owners. Let Putin thus help to finance the renaissance of NATO's raison d'être. Let him export their freedom-seeking innovators and entrepreneurs. We shall need the money. We should welcome the talent. Let them all come.

Russian immigration has thus struck a rather different tone and nature to the other regions we have surveyed. This is not the same story we have heard so far about the desperation of poverty – many Russians buy homes and take up residency here. Katerina Ukhankova, who provides boutique private office services to wealthy Russians, points out that 'most of the leading local banks, large law firms and estate agents now have special Russian departments to make sure the rich Russians get higher quality service'. Of course, not all migrating Russians are wealthy, but it is estimated that even the average Russian tourists and visitors spend at least £300 million a year – a quarter of a million Russians visit Britain annually, either on business or as tourists.

In recent years, Russians have become more and more prominent in the City of London. It is estimated that there are thousands of Russians employed in business and finance in London, one of the world's major financial centres. Reflecting this concentration of talent, several professional associations and clubs prosper, such as the Anglo-Russian Legal Association, the Russian MBA Group, the Russian Banking Group, and the Russian Insurance Club.

To date, Russians have tended *not* to favour settling in exclusive enclaves in London – a symptom of their wealth no doubt – but they are now spreading beyond London, and exceptions to this general rule have perhaps emerged of late. Russians appear drawn to the increasingly popular St George's Hill Estate in Weybridge, Surrey, as well as the equally leafy Wentworth in Berkshire. According to the *Financial Times*, Russian buyers account for more than 100 of the 430 properties in the latter estate, which nestles next to the exclusive, eponymous golf course. 'They are the main driver in the market,' said Simon Ashwell, a director at the Weybridge office of Savills, the estate agent. Half of sales on the estate so far this year – at an average price of £7 million – have gone to Russians. Yet even here, Russians tend to keep themselves to themselves. 'There appears to be little in the way of a local Russian social scene,' reports the *Financial Times*.

The main socialising that does occur appears to revolve around the Orthodox Church and various cultural events. But there are some high-profile nightspots that do appear to exert a strong magnetism for the Russian community – both resident and visiting. One such honey pot is Novikov – the pricey Mayfair eatery owned by the eponymous Arkady Novikov – where customers are lucky to escape without spending at least £200 for two, even at lunchtime. It is said that Novikov is where the beautiful come to feed. All are tall, tanned, buffed and botoxed. As *Time Out* puts it, 'Walking through the revolving glass doors, you're immediately confronted by a cacophony of people lounging around the reception-cum-bar area, a riot of sharp suits, tight dresses and champagne flutes.'

With respect to hedonism, there is also a widespread view that many Russian call girls are making a substantial living in London – and, for that matter, further afield across Britain. London escort sites tend to boast outsized portfolios of ladies who cater for Russian visitors. One such site, Diva Escorts, explains to its clients that, 'our London service operates from 10 a.m. until late, but please be aware that not all escorts will be available at all times' – one might term that 'demand and supply'. Prices start at £150 an hour and rise rapidly to over £300 an hour.

*　　*　　*

It is certainly the case that the Russian business community is attracted to London because of its established reputation for maintaining and observing high standards in company law and corporate governance. That's why the FTSE 100 mining concern ENRC, based in Kazakh, was obliged to delist from the London Stock Exchange in November 2013.

In the wake of the Crimea crisis, there was a further surge in investment in the London property market by Russia's elite – bankers, lawyers, doctors, businessmen and oligarchs – on account of their fears of spiralling political and economic unrest back home. Estate agent Jones Lang La Salle estimates that Russian money accounts for 7 per cent of all property (both new-build and Georgian) worth more than £1 million in the inner heart of the UK's capital. Russia's professional middle class are snapping up apartments of £1–2 million across central London in the belief that it represents an unrivalled hedge against uncertainty.

Those same Russians also often need a UK base in any case in order to visit their children who are at school – British public schools. Indeed, there are a battalion of specialists providing advice to Russians wishing to place their children in British independent schools. One such business is Kalid Private Office, which states that it 'can assist with many educational services including consultancy, selecting and securing school placement, tuition, guardianship and career advice' from its offices in Mayfair's Berkeley Square.

Russian pupils studying in UK private schools have tripled in the six years leading up to 2013 – the fastest-growing national group. This has accelerated as Russia's political environment grows more retrograde and spreads Russian links more widely than mere financial investment. Significantly, Russian demand for British boarding school places has greatly enhanced the quality of accommodation offered by many such schools – gone are the days of large dormitories and freezing-cold showers. As one example, Queen Ethelburga's College in Yorkshire, which attracts a lot of Chinese and Russians, provides students with 'modern boarding accommodation' that 'consists of smart and well-equipped bedrooms, the majority now with private bathrooms, all with flat-screen TVs , DVD players, telephones with voicemail, fridges, electric kettles, microwaves, air conditioning, trouser presses, room safes and ice-makers'.

In the tertiary sector of education there are a great many Russian students here, not just at the Russell Group universities, but also at less well-known institutions. This has provided a valuable source of income for British colleges and it has also tended to raise the universities' ratings, since Russian students, particularly those studying maths, science and engineering, tend to gain high marks. This has offset the unfortunate trend among the native British, who tend to avoid what are termed 'hard' subjects, such as physics.

Why should it matter where the wealthy choose to live? They are not isolated. The influx of well-heeled Russians has led to a boom in employment in the personal services sector of the economy. Both in London and in the pockets of the Home Counties, there has been a strong demand for property services, chauffeurs, gardeners and cooks (Roman Abramovich is said to employ twenty-eight servants at his Fyning Hill estate alone), although perhaps the greatest demand is for security and bodyguards.

*　*　*

As well as oligarchs from the Russian Federation, London has attracted plutocrats from other former Soviet republics. One of the most high profile is Azerbaijan, previously part of the USSR and noted for its oil and gas wealth. This is the country that made Calouste Gulbenkian rich as well as the Nobel brothers. It is currently experiencing a boom with considerable direct foreign investment, despite concerns over its human rights record.

Perhaps the most prominent Azeri in London is Leyla Aliyeva, the daughter of the President of Azerbaijan who was educated at Queen's College, London (as was her sister Arzu). Leyla, born in 1985, has now set up home in Britain with her husband, Russian singer Emin Agalarov – who is himself the son of a billionaire property tycoon – and it is Britain in which their two sons will be educated. They live in an expensive penthouse overlooking Hyde Park. Leyla is the editor-in-chief of *Baku*, a glossy magazine about Azerbaijan launched in 2011, published by Condé Nast in London.

Three of the richest in the latest *Sunday Times* Rich List hark from the former Soviet Union

Alisher Usmanov

A Muslim originally born in Uzbekistan. He made his estimated £13.3 billion fortune from mining and investment. Starting out as a manufacturer of plastic bags, Usmanov has accumulated a massive empire, making him Britain's richest man. Although he maintains a relatively low public profile, he owns John Paul Getty's former home at Sutton Place in Surrey, as well as a home in north London worth over £50 million – not forgetting almost a 30 per cent stake in Arsenal football club. He is reported to have donated more than £110 million to charity in 2012/13.

Alisher Usmanov.

Len Blavatnik

Estimated to be worth £11 billion in 2013. He divides his time between London and New York and owns – among many other assets – Warner Brothers, the world's third-largest record label. He was born in Odessa, Ukraine, but educated at Harvard and Columbia in New York. The Blavatnik Family Foundation has donated generously to a range of museums and good causes, notably the British Museum, the Tate Modern, the Royal Opera House and the National Portrait Gallery. A couple of years ago, it was announced that his foundation had given one of the largest ever donations, valued at around £75 million, to Oxford University in order to establish a new school of government.

Len Blavatnik.

Roman Abramovich

Known here as owner of Chelsea Football Club, he was the governor of the remote Russian province of Chukotka from 2000 to 2008, but is based in the UK (with many other homes worldwide). In England, he owns a number of homes including no fewer than three adjacent properties knocked together on Cheyne Walk – one of the most expensive streets in London. It is reckoned that he has spent over £1 billion on Chelsea FC since he bought the club in 2003.

Roman Abramovich.

Chapter 10

Con-fusion: has migration made a Greater Britain?

THIS IMMIGRANT STORY HAS TAKEN us on a long journey, from the hope-shorn slave markets of the Barbary Coast,
to the boardroom billions of Arsenal and Chelsea. We have
travelled with the pitiful diasporas of history's clamp-downs,
tyrannies, persecutions and pogroms. We have experienced the
vision of mobility that is the hallmark of the early European
Union and blinked in the dazzle of the spending bonanza that
comes with Arab Summers and Russian Love.

We have turned to immigrants for our nails to be varnished, for our fruit to be picked, for our buses to be driven, for our beds to be made, for our wounds to be nursed, for our buildings to be built, for our music to be a vibrant global export, for our food to be diverse and tasty – edible, even.

We have thanked our lucky stars, or more likely congratulated ourselves, for their immigrant innovation, for their immigrant wealth and for their immigrant spirit, that turns rags to riches. We have embraced and benefitted from the immigrant consistency of new ideas and the immigrant constancy of our old monarchs. In our minds, we have all stood proud on the highest sporting podiums, proud of our British achievement, proud of our distinctively British diversity.

It was not an accident but a consequence. We nurtured the love of Britain throughout our vast empire. We taught the whole world our English language. We came to represent – later rather than sooner, but nonetheless powerfully – the rights of all men, the rule of law, the dignity of aspiration, the freedom to think, the chance to speak such thought. We headed the charge sheet on slavery, but so too our better nature led the charge toward emancipation – and, in the end, a deeper and wider emancipation for all, not just slaves.

It took us centuries learning these vital pillars of civilisation, and yet we have been impatient in promoting these virtues abroad. We emigrated across the world, imposed upon it. We later travelled throughout the world and opened our minds to it. Then, in time, we taught and led it – inspired it.

And people all across the old empire – all over the world – have listened, learned and believed what they heard, took our values as their values and took our culture to their hearts. When they learned, they rejected the empire – but they have stayed to pay their respects, taste freedom, take opportunities, escape oppression, better themselves, live their dreams, and have their children educated in the epiphany that is the liberal manner.

So yes, they have come in large numbers, but largely in response to our explicit invitations – often, in fact, to answer our urgent appeals. Migrants merely make use of mechanisms our leaders created with their actions, their acts and their speeches. So yes, they fill our jobs – our otherwise vacant jobs for which we are too feebly unqualified or too fecklessly uninterested in – but we asked them to. Our politicians did. We did.

And we have seen that this journey is not new. It is not something that started recently; rather it merely has become easier. Migration is as old as our hills, as old as the trees. This pooling, merging and fusing has never *not* existed. It is part and parcel, weft and warp, head and heart of who we are.

So much so that it is in nearly everybody's blood. We only need dare to look. And when we do dare, we can all trace some foreign root. It is always there, but – conveniently for many – it is not always visible. We, the British people, are not who we think. We are British, for sure, but, then again, we are not. We are an amalgam: Britishness is diversity – it always has been.

We pretend otherwise. The truth does not always suit the

need of the moment. The same breed of politicians – who themselves employ the builders, nannies and constituency labourers, praise the doctors and welcome the donations – would have us believe otherwise. The political classes would have us close our eyes, close our minds, close our borders, close our souls. They pretend we are something we're not – they deny our history. They pretend immigration causes problems it does not. They place the blame, scape the goat and demean their own all-too-limited intelligence. They are increasingly hell-bent on populism, treading the precipitous path toward small-country separatism. They have ceased to lead, even to the point of denying their own individual histories. The only race they now wish to win is the race to seem more racist – more than before, more than the next guy.

It is down to everyone, this trend – no single politician is responsible – but for me it can be distilled in the cynical transition of Home Secretary Theresa May from theoretically modernising party leadership candidate (remember, it was that which prompted her to use the famous phrase 'nasty party', meaning something the Tories should modernise away from) to the reality of her personally championing the nastiest of hate campaigns. It was a campaign designed to foster divisiveness in immigrant communities and to attract unpaid-for publicity thanks to its essentially controversial nature. It was a policy that represents the dominance of electoral calculus over political leadership, placing party self-interest over political character and personal integrity. It was a policy endorsed by David Cameron and little-questioned by his MPs – they all speak the same code; they all understood the message and the nod; they wink the same wink.

Get real. Britain is beyond this, better than this. Most significantly, the true country – the real country – is beyond even multiculturalism.

Indeed, the term 'multiculturalism' was one that was coined in the '60s to apply very specifically to immigration from the New Commonwealth. It was not immigration but colour that caused multiculturalism to become a very lively subject. Culturist thinking never applied in the same way to immigration from Europe, white South Africa or China, even. Multiculturalism was a new language that was really a way of talking about black and Asian people without saying black and Asian people.

Of course there are multiple cultures, but they are overlapping, interrelated cultures – multiculturalism, on the other hand, emphasises differentness and favours a maintenance of historic identity over current identity. Most people who are descended from immigrants do not think of themselves as immigrant, nor are they particularly conscious of their complexion. This is not to say that people are not acutely aware of their heritage, but being black or Asian is not, in the longer term, what really defines people.

There are other stronger bonds between people, and not necessarily racial ones. Cultural bonds and bonds of identity – national identity, religious identity or social identity – are more important. I was born here, I was educated here, I live here, I vote here, and I have every right to be here. When I shave in the morning, I don't first think of myself being black any more than a UK-born Anglo-Scandinavian wakes up worrying about the price of herring and where to get the wood for a faster longboat. I feel British in every conceivable way, and no other explanation is required.

This is the common experience of people with a mixed origin. So what are people supposed to make of these Census forms, of these job interview forms, of these tax credit forms, which all force a definition? The constant inference from these forms is that you actually belong somewhere else – that you're not truly British. It's an accident of birth that you are here and this is why you need to be identified in such a way. Being British isn't good enough.

But this is a great challenge for somebody like me – and, in fact, for most people. There's an Afro-Caribbean box, an Indian box … but I am both and neither. I want to tick the British box, but I know that is not what they mean. Like so many others, I am a fusion. British culture is a fusion and I am a part of that.

I am not saying multiculturalism is meaningless or does not exist, but it is a concept that has greater meaning and purpose for first-generation immigrants. The descendants of immigrants have a mixed experience, and they quickly move beyond their cultural pigeonholes – grabbing or offering the best from both worlds. Multiculturalism is not an end in itself but the stepping stone to a greater fusion. A concentration of residence within

specific places facilitates self-help among immigrant populations – it eases the transition, shares the burden and overcomes
the language barrier. I have shown many such examples in
this book – as well as examples of the over-dissipation of new
immigration achieving the opposite of its intention, leading
to social isolation, stigma and, ultimately, failure.

However, the greater immigrant story lies not in these
communities, but right across the land. Unseen, unnoticed,
unremarked-upon – so long has this migration been taking
place and so deep in our genes has this fusion been entrenched,
that it is now part of us all.

We were, and still are, quick to emigrate, unquestioning of
its value. Of course, emigration is a benefit to the destination
country always and everywhere – is it not? We perceive ourselves to be God's gift as emigrants abroad, but have decried
the immigrant at home.

Yet emigration is immigration seen from the other side.
What is a benefit in one direction is equally a benefit in the
other. When we decry immigration, we deny our own nature.

If you close your eyes for a moment and look at the huge
canvas of the history of the British Isles, you would see many
things. There would be an astonishing amount of traffic in and
out of our ports; thousands of boats, ships and planes; millions of people, year after year, century after century; ceaseless
comings and goings, building and forming the country and
its physical and psychological culture.

It's a fantastic story; a fusion story; a Britain greater than the sum of its parts. A small country of breathtaking, unparalleled success – in significant part because it has opened itself up to external influence and infusion. It is a country to which we all belong.

Acknowledgements

P. G. WODEHOUSE ONCE ASKED why a friend required a long explanation for writing a book, when a simple apology would do. The only apology I owe is to my publishers for delivering my manuscript late. I am sorry, Iain. The apology stops there. I also owe him and his formidable team – Olivia and Melissa especially – an enormous thank you for agreeing to publish my book.

This book is entirely my idea. Like King Lear, I am a sucker for self-inflicted punishment. A number of good friends told me not to attempt it, but they have, nonetheless, stood shoulder to shoulder with me, and have been invaluable along the way. Together we have poured over drafts, agreed, disagreed and debated many issues as we went along. I hope the outcome will stand the test of time and make a balancing contribution to a subject that is being soured by the right as they once again march towards their tiresome vision of an isolated nation of lonely delusional purity. If they ever get there, the shock that not a single one of their perceived problems has gone away will be truly wondrous.

Keith Adams has been a lifelong friend. He is quietly brilliant and politically astute and I have known him since he was an undergraduate along with Michael Gove at Oxford. He told me even back then, as we all walked through the Somerset countryside, that Gove would be in the Cabinet but would probably be too radical for his own good. Keith and I both worked in politics together. He became a special advisor, a contemporary of Cameron and Osborne in that role, but always idiosyncratically green and independent within that scene. Almost unbelievably, we both stood at the Downing Street window, next to Mrs Thatcher, silently looking down at that unforgettable blizzard of flashbulbs the day she left No. 10. His young sons Tycho and Boris have curiously monitored this project, and they themselves are already furiously writing. Sadly, they won't show anyone what they have written, but I shall look out for them in ten years or so.

To complete the circle, allow me to mention Winifred Adeyemi. She has been an extraordinary researcher, always lively and enthusiastic, a ceaseless ferment of global culture. Her contribution can be felt throughout.

Keith Boyfield is an economist, friend and bon vivant and we spent many hours on this topic in the Reform Club, where we are both members. His invaluable wisdom (he has written a few books before) and tireless energy in going over drafts and providing statistical data made this book possible. Alongside them both stands Dr Alice Sheridan. Alice is a no-nonsense academic, who has a way of illuminating the soul and throwing light and shade into various chapters – it was her idea that I should include, at the eleventh hour, a chapter on Ireland.

Last, but by no means least, is the University of Cambridge Library. I spent hours there and the book-lined walls gave me inspiration to finish the job.

Thank you to everyone and to the many whom time does not allow me to mention.

Index

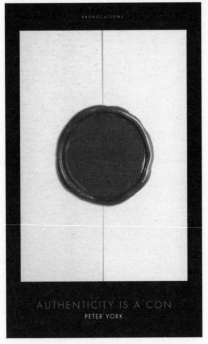

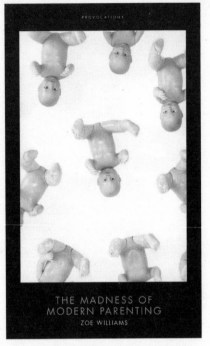